When?

Thinking Through the Olivet Prophecy

Stan Way

WESTBOW
PRESS®
A DIVISION OF THOMAS NELSON
& ZONDERVAN

WestBow Press books may be ordered through booksellers or by contacting:

WestBow Press
A Division of Thomas Nelson & Zondervan
1663 Liberty Drive
Bloomington, IN 47403
www.westbowpress.com
1 (866) 928-1240

Scripture quotations are from the ESV® Bible (The Holy Bible, English
Standard Version®), copyright © 2001 by Crossway, a publishing ministry
of Good News Publishers. Used by permission. All rights reserved.

ISBN: 978-1-9736-5788-0 (sc)
ISBN: 978-1-9736-5787-3 (e)

Print information available on the last page.

WestBow Press rev. date: 4/24/2019

About the Author

Stan Way (B.S., Pastoral Theology, Bethany University) has been active in Christian ministry for fifty years and is currently serving as Pastor Emeritus of Cornerstone Christian Church in Medford, Oregon. He is also a member of the adjunct faculty of Pacific Bible College (Medford, Oregon).

Contents

Preface

Perhaps one of the most discussed and debated sections of the Gospels is the 'Olivet Prophecy' of Jesus found in Matthew 24, Mark 13, and Luke 21. What does it tell us about the coming of Christ? How should we understand Jesus' prediction that "...this generation will not pass away until all these things take place (Matt.24:34)?" Over the years, there have been a number of differing understandings presented to us. Some say that Jesus is describing events that will occur just prior to his second coming. He is describing events that are still in the future. Other scholars are convinced that Jesus is speaking of two events. He is describing the fall of Jerusalem and the destruction of the Temple in 70 A.D., as well as predicting his second coming at the end of the current dispensation. And then, there are those who hold to a preterist position, claiming that Jesus is speaking only of the 70 A.D. event. Of one thing we can be sure: all the positions taken can be wrong, but they can't all be right.

I was raised in a denomination that was committed to Dispensational theology and taught that the 'Olivet Prophecy' was describing events yet to take place. In the United States this is the most public and prominent position held today, and it has opened the door to speculations about the return of Christ. Some have even set dates for the second coming based on their understanding of the 'this generation' statement made by Jesus. By using the establishment of the Jewish State in 1948 as a 'start-point' in calculating a generation (40 years biblically), many believed that Christ would return in or before 1988. This didn't occur, so a new 'start-point' was established. The Arab-Israeli Six Day War in 1967 seemed appropriate because Israel gained sole control of Jerusalem. The prophecy experts again predicted that the second coming of Christ would occur within the next 40 years. But, 2007 passed and we're still waiting for Christ's return. Where do we go from here? Is there another viable 'start-point' for our calculations? No. It seems that we should revisit our understanding of the 'Olivet Prophecy'. History is telling us that the futurist interpretation of the prophecy is wrong.

The fact that all the speculations and predictions have proven to be misguided carries some serious pastoral concerns. Is biblical prophecy reliable? Is the Bible a true revelation from God? Is our expectation of Christ's return a legitimate Christian hope? My concern is that a misguided interpretation of this important prophecy can undermine the faith of some sincere Christian believers. It can also be a point of proof used by those hostile to the gospel to support their claim that the Bible is not divine revelation; it's not God's Word. This should concern all of us as faithful followers of Christ!

There is an interpretation of the 'Olivet Prophecy' that I'm convinced preserves its integrity and demonstrates the reliability of biblical prophecy. The understanding that I'm presenting for your consideration is that Jesus was predicting the fall of Jerusalem and the destruction of the Temple that occurred in 70 A.D. This event brought the Jewish Age to an observable end. Jesus was not predicting his second coming at the end of human history, he was describing his coming in judgment on Apostate Israel before many of his original hearers passed from the scene. This is prophecy now fulfilled!

Stan Way

Acknowledgments

Whe it comes to biblical prophecy it is unwise to claim understandings that are new. Private interpretations that are not supported by biblical scholars, both past and present, should be rejected. The understanding of the 'Olivet Prophecy' that I am presenting in this book is not mine alone, it is a position long-held by many in the church. My convictions have been shaped by the insights and understandings of other faithful Christians and biblical scholars. I am grateful for the challenging and stimulating conversations I've had over the years with my colleagues at Cornerstone Christian Church. Their understanding of the Bible and insights into biblical prophecy have been a tremendous help in shaping my convictions. Also, the historical works of Josephus and Eusebius have confirmed, in my mind, the truthfulness of Jesus' 'Olivet' predictions. In addition, I deeply appreciate the research done by Gary DeMar and published in his book *Last Days Madness*. Many of the historical citations I've included in my book are sourced in his work. The scholarly work of many has provided insight into the prophecy of Jesus preserved for us in his 'Olivet Discourse'. It is the careful work of others that has given birth to my small contribution to the prophetic discussion.

Introduction –
'The Prophetic Voice'

Prophecy played an extremely important role in the history and religious life of Israel; so much so that Israel's religion and history are fundamentally prophetic. When you read through the Old Testament literature you hear a prophetic voice that speaks to the real historical events of the people of God. In fact, it is fair to say that Old Testament prophecy flows out of Israel's historical experiences. We see this at its very beginnings with the call of Abraham (Gen.12). God sovereignly broke into Abram's life, revealed himself, and called him to leave his country and follow God's leading to a 'promised land'. Abram's told that if he is obedient to God's call he will be the father of a great nation and all nations would be blessed because of him. This relatedness of prophecy to history is one feature of Israel's religion that made it distinctively different from the pagan religions of the nations around her.

Israel's religious understanding was rooted in prophetic revelation that spoke to real events and issues that faced them as a people. It was always timely and relevant, and came by way of divinely appointed prophets rather than human speculation, superstition, or cultic practices. God made himself known to them through prophetic revelation that shaped the events of their national life. For this reason, the historical books of Joshua, Judges, 1&2 Samuel and 1&2 Kings are called the 'Former Prophets' in the Hebrew scriptures. These books demonstrate that the history of Israel was, in itself, a revelation of God. It was prophetic!

Prophecy, then, holds an essential and prominent place in the Old Testament witness. It confronts us with the character and will of God. It presents God as the 'Lord of history', the one who controls the events and flow of history for an ultimate purpose; the fulfillment of God's redemptive promise and the establishment of his kingdom, his sovereign rule upon the earth. This is where the flow of human history will ultimately end, with the full, unhindered manifestation of God's rule. This is clearly anticipated by the prophet Zechariah -

> *"On that day living waters shall flow out from Jerusalem, half of them to the eastern sea and half of them to the western sea. It shall continue in summer as in winter. And the Lord will be king over all the earth. On that day the Lord will be one and his name one (Zech.14:8,9)."*

Generally speaking, then, Old Testament prophecy was the means by which God spoke to Israel, addressing its present needs and establishing its future hope.

The Nature and Function of Old Testament Prophecy

Some scholars have suggested that Israel's prophetic institution was the result of its embracing and refining the cultic practices of its pagan neighbors. But the scripture does not support this notion at all. Moses spoke to this when instructing Israel before they entered the land of promise. He told them that they were not to 'follow the abominable practices' of the nations that occupied the land. In fact, they were to drive these nations out of the land because of their abominations (Deut.18:9-22).

Clearly, biblical prophecy is not a refined form of pagan practices; those are condemned. What Moses says is that God would raise up a succession of prophets who would declare the messages of God, and that this office would one day culminate in the arrival of one great Prophet like himself (Deut.18:15). The New Testament witness is that this promise of a coming 'great prophet' was fulfilled in Christ. The Hebrew prophets, then, came on the scene because of God's call and they were not practicing a refined form of pagan divination.

This being the case, how should we define and understand the function of biblical prophecy? The noun, prophet, means spokesman or speaker. The verb, 'to prophecy', means 'to flow', 'to bubble forth' or 'to pour forth words'. The classic passage that clarifies the meaning of 'prophet' is found in Exodus 7, verses 1&2 - " And the Lord said to Moses, "See, I have made you like God to Pharaoh, and your brother Aaron shall be your prophet. You shall speak all that I command you, and your brother Aaron shall tell Pharaoh to let the people of Israel go out of his land." According to this, the function of the prophet is to deliver a message from God. They are to be God's 'mouth-piece' or 'spokesman'. They simply say what God has said, and to fail in this is to be a false prophet.

Three-Fold Ministry

When you survey the prophetic material in the Old Testament, you discover that the prophets in Israel exercised a three-fold ministry. First, they expounded and interpreted the Mosaic revelation. They had a strong connection to the Mosaic Covenant. John Calvin spoke to this issue when he wrote - "...to trace the Prophets to the law, from which they derived their doctrine, like streams from a fountain...so that they may be justly held...to be its interpreters...Thus when the Prophets inculcate moral duties, they bring forward nothing new, but only explain those parts of the Law which had been misunderstood"[1]. The Prophets were divinely appointed moral and ethical preachers. They spoke to their contemporaries and called for godly living that conformed to the Covenant vision. They spoke out against idolatry, infidelity, oppression, and iniquity, as well as social, moral, and political corruption. Primarily, biblical prophecy takes the form of 'forth-telling': proclaiming God's word under the anointing of the Holy Spirit to the prophet's own generation. Yet, often woven into their ethical preaching are predictions of future events. These events concerned Israel, the Gentile nations, and the coming Messianic Age. Biblical prophecy, then, also contains predictive elements; and yet, the predictions of future events were never merely to demonstrate that God knows the future or to satisfy man's curiosity about future things. On the whole, the predictive elements of prophecy are rooted in, and projected out from, the moral and spiritual condition of God's people at the time. These predictions typically speak of coming judgment, salvation, or the Messiah and his kingdom. The biblical scholar and commentator,

---

[1] John Calvin, 'Preface to the Prophet Isaiah', Commentary on Isaiah, Vol.1 (Christian Classics Ethereal Library, Grand Rapids, MI, 1999).

R.B.Y. Scott, writes - "Their prophecies express their moral certainty and spiritual understanding of what will be because of what is..."[2]. It is proper to say, then, that biblical prophecy also takes the form of 'foretelling'.

Watchmen and Guardians of the Covenant

The third ministry expression of the prophets is that they were watchmen and guardians of the Covenant. They warned the people of the dangers of religious apostasy, confronting them regarding their covenant commitments. The historical situation facing the classical prophets of the 8th - 6th centuries B.C. brought this ministry to the forefront. The conditions that confronted the Prophets were severe and troubling. The Kingdom was divided. The Northern tribes had accepted calf worship; Baal worship had been introduced during the reign of Ahab. In the South, apostasy was the result of foreign alliances and the inter-marriage of God's covenant people with pagans. A prime example of this was the marriage of Ahab and Jezebel's daughter to Jehoram, the King of Judah (2 Kings 8). Also, the priests had abandoned their calling and fallen into sin.

The Prophets were to warn and turn the nation away from its sin and apostasy, back to keeping the Covenant. So, the purpose of the Prophets' prophetic ministry was to sound the alarm and warn of approaching spiritual peril, while calling for spiritual purity. The Prophet was a watchman, a guardian of the Covenant. Old Testament Prophets, then, were preachers (forth-tellers), predictors (fore-tellers), and watchmen (guardians of the Covenant).

Since prophecy has such a prominent role in the biblical witness, it is relevant and has something to say to us today. We need to examine it carefully. Again, R.B.Y. Scott speaks insightfully to this point - "They speak, not of our age but to it, because the Word of God is in their mouth. Through their literary remains in the Old Testament we make contact with living men, rich and deep and powerful men, observant, sympathetic and in deadly earnest. They understand human nature and the human predicament. They feel the urgent meaning of history as the sphere of man's moral decisions and of God's participation in the conflict of human wills. They know God as the fount of meaning in the context of everyday life; and they find the reality of his presence in the inner world of their own spirits. Such men must be significant for religion in every age" [3].

---

[2] R.B.Y. Scott, *The Relevance of the Prophets* (Macmillan Publishing Co., New York, N.Y., 1944), p.14.
[3] Ibid., p.216.

CHAPTER 1
Prophetic Patterns & Themes

When you think of prophecy, what is the first thing that comes to your mind? Perhaps your initial response to this question is shaped by the prevailing understanding of prophecy which focuses on future-telling, with particular reference to 'end of the world' speculations and scenarios, which usually involve a much anticipated divine inbreaking that brings judgment on the wicked and deliverance to the righteous. This understanding is not unique to our generation; it is actually a 'pre-Christian' understanding that dominated and defined the expectations of many Jews at the time of Christ. You can hear this in the questions posed by Christ's disciples, "...what will be the sign of your coming and of the close of the age (Matt. 24:3)?..." "...Lord, will you at this time restore the kingdom to Israel (Acts 1:6)?" The disciples were curious about the end of the Age - were they at the close of one Epoch and the beginning of another? This became part of the Christian expectation early on, and rightly so, because Christ had promised to come again.

But there are always some who develop an unhealthy preoccupation with this aspect of Christian teaching. For example, in the 2nd century AD a charismatic figure by the name of Montanus became quite influential. He lived in Phrygia (Asia Minor) and claimed to be a prophet, and to have received new revelation. He said that Christ would return soon, and that the heavenly Jerusalem would descend on Phrygia. Christ would then rule the world from there for a thousand years. Individuals making claims of special revelation or special insight into biblical prophecy are part of the Christian landscape in every generation, even today. In a publication released in 1992 by the 'Mission for the Coming Days', located in San Jose, California, the prediction was made that the 'rapture' of the Church would take place on October 28, 1992. Harold Camping, founder of 'Family Radio' in the San Francisco Bay area, said that the second coming of Christ would occur in the fall of 1994. Grant Jeffrey, in his book, *Armageddon: Appointment With Destiny*, calculated that Christ would return in the year 2000. None of these predictions proved to be true.

These false predictions raise a fundamental question: does this preoccupation with 'end of the world speculations' represent a proper handling of biblical prophecy? Perhaps a good way to consider and answer this question is to look at the patterns and themes found in the Minor Prophets. Do these current 'end of the world' predictions conform to the function of prophecy as we find it in the Old Testament Prophets? If pressed, I would have to say "no". Does this, then, mean that the scripture is silent regarding the end-point of human history? No. Scripture speaks to this question, but it is a minor theme, not a major one. The end of human history, as we understand it, is typically addressed in the context of a larger discussion regarding resurrection and the full manifestation of God's redemptive work in the world. The focus of the Christian gospel is on the cross, salvation, the new life we have in Christ, and the bodily resurrection of believers at the end of the Age. Actually, when biblical prophecy is considered in its historical context, it is far more focused on the present than the future.

Patterns & Themes

Let me underscore some of the prominent patterns and themes of prophecy presented in the work of the Minor Prophets. First, biblical prophecy majors in 'forth-telling' and minors in 'foretelling'. By definition, a prophet is God's spokesman speaking under the inspiration and direction of the Holy Spirit. As mentioned in the Introduction, a biblical prophet is primarily a moral and ethical preacher. He exposes the moral corruption and spiritual bankruptcy of the people to whom he is called to preach. There is always an element of impending judgment in his preaching, and a constant call to repentance. This is the major form of prophecy found in the Bible. According to Dr. Gordon Fee, less than 2% of Old Testament prophecy is messianic, less than 5% describes the New Covenant age, and less that 1% concerns events yet to come[1]. Dr. William LaSor, former Old Testament Professor Emeritus at Fuller Theological Seminar, puts this in perspective - "By simply picking verses from the prophets and pasting them together to give 'prophecies that prove the Bible' or 'Jesus Christ in prophecy,' one creates the impression that prophecy is 'history written in advance.' However, when one studies the prophets, this glamorous concept suddenly disappears. It is necessary to plow through chapters that have nothing to do with the future in order to find a single verse, or even part of a verse, that is 'prophecy.'[2] Yet, there is predictive prophecy (prophetic foretelling) found in the Bible. It is certainly present in the Minor Prophets; they spoke of coming judgment and future restoration. This is a very impressive aspect of biblical prophecy. There is real, verifiable prediction and fulfillment found in the Bible. But the predictive elements of the prophet's preaching were never unrelated to the current conditions they were addressing. Dr. LaSor went on to say - "On exceptional occasions, he [God] gives rather precise details about what he is going to do. Yet even in this instruction, usually called 'predictive prophecy,' the predictive element almost always is firmly attached to the present situation. The prophet speaks about what has meaning for his listeners. He does not suddenly forget them and utter an irrelevant 'prophecy of things to come.' Rather, he takes them from that moment into the sweep of divine redemptive activity and centers on a truth that will become a beacon to God's people."[3] So, biblical prophecy majors in forth-telling and minors in foretelling.

Also, biblical prophecy affirms God's transcendence and sovereignty over all nations. This is a recurring theme in the Prophets, both Major and Minor, and is a radical departure from the prevailing henotheism of the day. The idea that one could give allegiance to a tribal god while acknowledging the existence of other gods is foreign to the Bible. The Prophets proclaimed that there is only one God [YHWH], the God of the Hebrews, and all nations are under his authority and accountable to him. For example, Amos affirms this by listing a series of judgments on the Gentile nations that

---

[1] Gordon Fee, *How to Read the Bible for All Its Worth* (Zondervan, 2003), p. 150.

[2] William LaSor, *Old Testament Survey* (Eerdman), p.304-305.

[3] Ibid., p.305..

CHAPTER 2

Framing the Prophetic Picture

Malachi chapter four is a classic piece of Old Testament prophecy. For the Jews, it was the final prophetic message they would hear for four hundred plus years -

"For behold, the day is coming, burning like an oven, when all the arrogant and all evildoers will be stubble. The day that is coming shall set them ablaze, says the Lord of hosts, so that it will leave them neither root nor branch. But for you who fear my name, the sun of righteousness shall rise with healing in its wings. You shall go out leaping like calves from the stall. And you shall tread down the wicked, for they will be ashes under the soles of your feet, on the day when I act, says the Lord of hosts. "Remember the law of my servant Moses, the statutes and rules that I commanded him at Horeb for all Israel. "Behold, I will send you Elijah the prophet before the great and awesome day of the Lord comes. And he will turn the hearts of fathers to their children and the hearts of children to their

fathers, lest I come and strike the land with a decree of utter destruction (Mal.4:1-6)."

This is true prophecy; there is warning of coming judgment, there is a call to repentance, reassurance is given to the obedient, and there is a predictive element - "Behold, I will send you Elijah the prophet before the great and awesome day of the Lord comes (v.5)." For that generation of Jews, this disturbing warning of coming judgment was left ringing in their ears; and then, the prophetic voice fell silent, not to be heard again for four hundred years. This ends the Old Testament record of Jewish history. And yet, the period between the Old and New Testaments shaped the Jewish mindset and world view that confronted Jesus in the first century A.D.

The Inter-testamental Period

Given the importance of the 'inter-testamental' period in shaping Jewish attitudes and expectations, it is important to have at least a general knowledge of the period. There is one word that probably best describes this period of Jewish history...'occupation'. Palestine was a political pawn subjected to a series of foreign occupations. It was a dark and very difficult season. And yet, in reality, it was part of a prophetic unfolding. Daniel had already sketched it out while living among the Jewish exiles in Babylon and serving in the king's courts. King Nebuchadnezzar had a very disturbing dream; it was a vision of future things. The vision deeply troubled the king because he didn't understanding its meaning. But God revealed the dream to Daniel and gave him the interpretation of its meaning. The dream and Daniel's understanding of it is profound. What Daniel saw was a great image with a head of gold, chest and arms of silver, mid-section and thighs of bronze, legs of iron, and feet made of iron and clay. Then Daniel said that Nebuchadnezzar saw a stone, without human origin, that struck the feet of the image, and it crumbled into pieces and was blown away by the wind. The stone then became a 'great mountain and filled the whole earth' (Dan.2:35). Daniel went on to interpret the dream for the King. What Nebuchadnezzar saw in this dream was the rise and fall of coming kingdoms (Dan.2:31-47).

A Prophetic Preview

What is presented in Nebuchadnezzar's dream is a prophetic preview of future world powers, and an affirmation that God's rule will prevail.

Nebuchadnezzar saw one great image with four distinct expressions. It speaks of human political power, the rule of human government. It pictures the political realities the Jews were experiencing then, and would continue to experience in the future. These were political powers that resist God's purposes and persecute God's people. But, the powers of this earth will not ultimately deter the 'rule of God'.

The four parts of the statue represent four kingdoms. The first, 'the head of gold', is Babylon. Daniel said to the King, "...you are that head of gold (v.38)." There is a companion to this in Daniel chapter seven, where Babylon is presented as a 'lion'. Babylon ruled over Palestine from 605-539B.C. The second kingdom presented as the 'chest and arms of silver' is the Medo-Persian Empire that ruled Palestine from 538-334 B.C. In chapter seven, it is the Bear. The statue's 'belly and thighs of bronze' represent Greece that ruled over the Jews from 333-142 B.C. And Daniel's vision gives an important detail related to the Greek occupation - "After this I looked, and behold, another, like a leopard, with four wings of a bird on its back. And the beast had four heads, and dominion was given to it (Dan.7:6)." With the death of Alexander the Great in 323 B.C. his empire was broken into four separate kingdoms, each ruled by one of his generals. The two that directly impacted Palestine were Ptolemy and Seleucus. Palestine was ruled by the Ptolemies for one hundred years and the Seleucid Empire annexed Palestine in 198 B.C. They ruled the region until the Maccabean rebellion won a fragile independence for the Jews, first religiously in 164 B.C. and then politically in 142 B.C. This lasted until the Romans conquered the region in B.C. 63. The Romans are represented by the 'legs of iron' and the feet of 'iron and clay'. In Daniel seven, Rome is the 'fourth beast' with 'large iron teeth'. But the Empire had feet of 'iron and clay' that ultimately brought it down. Rome's lack of internal integrity caused it to collapse. In decline for two hundred years, Rome is finally brought to its knees in 476 A.D.

A Hopeful Note

In the midst of this dark prophetic description of the future, there is a hopeful note. The much anticipated 'Kingdom of God' [God's rule] would ultimately prevail. There are clear references to this in Daniel chapters two and seven -

*"And in the days of those kings the God of heaven will
set up a kingdom that shall never be destroyed, nor shall
the kingdom be left to another people. It shall break in
pieces all these kingdoms and bring them to an end, and
it shall stand forever, just as you saw that a stone was
cut from a mountain by no human hand, and that it
broke in pieces the iron, the bronze, the clay, the silver,
and the gold. A great God has made known to the king
what shall be after this. The dream is certain, and its
interpretation sure (Dan.2:44,45)."... "there came one like
a son of man and he came to the Ancient of Days and was
presented before him. And to him was given dominion
and glory and a kingdom, that all peoples, nations, and
languages should serve him; his dominion is an everlasting
dominion, which shall not pass away, and his kingdom
one that shall not be destroyed. "As for me, Daniel, my
spirit within me was anxious, and the visions of my head
alarmed me. I approached one of those who stood there
and asked him the truth concerning all this. So he told me
and made known to me the interpretation of the things.
'These four great beasts are four kings who shall arise out
of the earth. But the saints of the Most High shall receive
the kingdom and possess the kingdom forever, forever and
ever (Dan.7:13-18)."*

The over-arching point of these visions is that world powers will rise
and fall, resist God's rule, and persecute God's people; but ultimately they
cannot destroy God's purposes or God's people. Why? Because the 'Son of
Man' will be given sovereign power and all nations will worship him; his
rule will not pass away and his kingdom will never be destroyed (Dan.7:14).
The 'Kingdom of God' will ultimately assert itself and capture the hearts
and minds of people from every race and nation through the saving work
of Christ, who is the 'Son of Man'. There is great hope here; God's rule will
be established, and the Jewish expectation will be fulfilled.

It is this expectation, while experiencing extended political oppression,
that transformed the Jewish understanding of how the Kingdom of God
would be established. The hope of freeing themselves and conquering their
enemies militarily gave way to the expectation of a dramatic apocalyptic

in-breaking of God on their behalf. The Messiah would deliver them! During the Monarchy, under David and Solomon, the conviction was that the 'rule of God' would be established through the power and expansion of the kingdom of Israel. But after the Monarchy was divided and destroyed, this expectation was abandoned. The only possible way for the Kingdom of God to be established and for the kingdom of Israel to be restored was through supernatural, divine intervention. It is this political and religious environment that gave birth to the 'Apocalyptic' movement [2nd century B.C.-2nd century A.D.]. This movement produced a very unique and colorful body of literature. The prophetic voice was dead, but the Apocalyptic vision was very much alive. Apocalyptic language is a language of crisis, and it presents its ideas in very dramatic terms. D.S. Russell, in his book *Apocalyptic: Ancient and Modern*, describes his first reading of Apocalyptic literature - "I found myself in a weird and wonderful world of fantasy and dreams - beasts with sprouting horns, dragons spouting fire, falling stars, mysterious horsemen, mystical mountains, sacred rivers, devastating earthquakes, fearsome giants, demon progeny, monstrous births, portents in heaven, portents on earth. Its often frenzied and frenetic descriptions of coming woes sounded like the product of over-heated minds."[1] This literature is non-canonical and not accepted as scripture; and yet, we have prophecy in the Bible that uses Apocalyptic language and imagery. For example, we see it used in Daniel, Ezekiel, Zechariah, Revelation, and the Olivet Discourse. But what the use of this literary form does for us is helps us understand the Messianic expectations and world view of the majority of Jews of Jesus' day (see 2 Esdras 12:31-34; 13:37-40). It was this kind of Apocalyptic material that fueled the Jews' Messianic hopes.

Even though Apocalyptic language is used in biblical prophecy, the two prophetic forms are distinctly different. Biblical prophecy is characterized by 'forth-telling' [moral preaching] as its majority expression and also includes related 'fore-telling' [predictive elements]. Its primary message is impending judgment coupled with a call to repentance. Its overall tone is pessimistic. Apocalyptic literature, on the other hand, focuses on divine intervention and deliverance rather than moral condemnation. It anticipates the end of oppression and the establishment of the Kingdom [rule] of God. Apocalyptic literature was a source of comfort and hope to

[1] D.S. Russel, *Apocalyptic: Ancient and Modern* (Hayward Lectures & Nordenhaug Memorial Lectures), SCM Press, 2012, p. 1.

an oppressed people. Its message was communicated through dramatic language filled with numbers, symbols, and striking images. The message it delivered was optimistic; it presented a hope-filled vision of the future. A.S. Peake, in his book, *The Relevance of Apocalyptic*, summarizes the difference between biblical prophecy and Apocolyptic prophecy very succinctly - "Speaking generally, the prophets foretold the future that should arise out of the present, while the Apocalyptists foretold the future that should break into the present."[2] The Prophets spoke of present sin which would bring future judgment; the Apocalyptists spoke of present tribulation into which would come divine deliverance.

This was the environment into which Jesus came, and which the early church was called to confront. Israel was an occupied nation and an oppressed people who had forgotten the last prophetic message given to them by Malachi, which was a stern warning that the 'great and dreadful day of the Lord' was coming. This was the next major event on the divine calendar for Israel - not deliverance. And yet, they were anticipating Messianic intervention and the rebirth of Israel's 'Golden Age'. It was a mistake; Jerusalem was about to be judged!

---

[2] A.S Peake, *The Relevance of Apocalyptic*, p. 38'

CHAPTER 3

The Prophetic
Silence is Broken

There is a flow to history, and often the pressing issues and urgent events of one generation lose their prominence and are forgotten by the next generation. As a result, there is an absence of historical perspective and reference points to help emerging generations deal with new demands and personal challenges. This is certainly true when you review the history of the Jews. For example, the dominant theme of Malachi's prophecy had been largely forgotten or ignored by the Jews of Jesus' day. Malachi had warned of coming judgment. The judgment was going to be severe; so severe that he referred to it as the 'great and dreadful day of the Lord' (Mal.4:5). So, Malachi was warning Israel and calling the people to return to covenant faithfulness. But four hundred years had passed and the Jews had endured one foreign occupation after another. The prophetic call to national repentance had been replaced by an expectation of apocalyptic intervention. They were anticipating the dramatic rebirth of Israel's 'Golden Age' brought about by the arrival and earthly reign of Messiah.

There are some pertinent points made in Malachi's prophecy that are worth additional consideration. In chapter three, Malachi says that a 'messenger' would be sent to serve as a forerunner of the Lord, who was going to execute judgment on Jerusalem and the Temple. This judgment was going to be severe and it would alter the religious life of Israel forever. God's warning is very descriptive - "But who can endure the day of his coming, and who can stand when he appears? For he is like a refiner's fire and like fullers' soap (Mal.3:2)." The judgment that was coming was because of apostate Israel's ungodliness, rebelliousness, and persistent sinning - "Then I will draw near to you for judgment. I will be a swift witness against the sorcerers, against the adulterers, against those who swear falsely, against those who oppress the hired worker in his wages, the widow and the fatherless, against those who thrust aside the sojourner, and do not fear me, says the Lord of hosts (Mal.3:5)." In chapter four, Malachi continues to develop this judgment theme by using very descriptive judgment language. He says that a day was coming that would burn like an oven, and it would consume "all the arrogant and all evildoers" (Mal.4:1). Malachi goes on to say - "The day that is coming shall set them ablaze (v.1)". This is a disturbing picture of judgment that will involve fire, death, and devastating destruction. And yet, in the midst of the judgment there is a hopeful message of deliverance. For those who reverence God, "the sun of righteousness shall rise with healing in its wings (v.2)." Those who take the prophetic warnings seriously will escape the judgment.

However, the images of 'refiner's fire' and 'burning like an oven' in reference to the Lord's coming are the language of judgment, not deliverance. In large part the Jews of the first century AD had turned their backs on the prophet's message and embraced the far more encouraging and comforting apocalyptic vision of the future. So there was an urgent need for a fresh prophetic voice to challenge this false vision, especially if they were on the eve of the fulfillment of Malachi's prophecy.

The Time Marker

Could this be the case? Was judgment close? Yes. Malachi had given a clear 'time marker' to look for - "Behold, I send my messenger, and he will prepare the way before me (Mal.3:1)"..."Behold, I will send you Elijah the prophet before the great and awesome [dreadful] day of the Lord comes (Mal.4:5)." The Lord would send a messenger of preparation more precisely, the prophet Elijah, with a message of repentance. The New Testament gospels present John the Baptist as the fulfillment of Malachi's prophecy. He is the forerunner, the prophet like Elijah who would appear on the eve of the 'great and dreadful day of the Lord'. This is what Jesus taught -

"As they went away, Jesus began to speak to the crowds concerning John: "What did you go out into the wilderness to see? A reed shaken by the wind? What then did you go out to see? A man dressed in soft clothing? Behold, those who wear soft clothing are in kings' houses. What then did you go out to see? A prophet? Yes, I tell you, and more than a prophet. This is he of whom it is written, "Behold, I send my messenger before your face, who will prepare your way before you" Truly, I say to you, among those born of women there has arisen no one greater than John the Baptist. Yet the one who is least in the kingdom of heaven is greater than he. From the days of John the Baptist until now the kingdom of heaven has suffered violence, and the violent take it by force. For all the Prophets and the Law prophesied until John, and if you are willing to accept it, he is Elijah who is to come (Matt.11:7-14; see also Matt.17:10-13; Lk.1:11-17,67-80)."

It is clear that the gospel writers were convinced that John the Baptist fulfilled Malachi's prophecy about Elijah's reappearance. God's grace had delayed judgment for over four hundred years, but the clock of judgment was ticking again. The prophetic silence was about to be broken.

With the arrival of John the Baptist on the public stage, the voice of a true biblical prophet was heard again. His public ministry was built around the classic features of an Old Testament prophet: moral preaching, and a call to repentance coupled with a predictive element. John preached a message that was straightforward and very confrontational - "Repent, for the kingdom of heaven is at hand [near] (Matt.3:2)." He was the one fulfilling Isaiah's prophecy - "The voice of one crying in the wilderness: 'Prepare the way of the Lord; make his paths straight (Matt.3:3; Isa.40:3)." Apparently, John was a striking figure, and by the hundreds, people came to hear him preach. In response to his message, they were confessing their sins and expressing public repentance through baptism. According to Isaiah and Malachi, this long awaited prophet would have a twofold ministry: he would be the forerunner of the coming Savior (Isa.40:3), and the one who would appear just before judgment would be executed against Jerusalem and the Temple (Mal.3:1-2; 4:1-5).

John's message was the one they had been waiting to hear for centuries. The 'kingdom (basileia) of heaven', the dynamic rule of God, was near. This phrase 'is at hand' carries the idea of 'has come'. From the Jews' apocalyptic perspective, John's announcement meant that the political oppression and foreign occupation was almost over. In preparation, John was calling them to repent, to turn from their sin and compromised lives, and return to covenant faithfulness. This understanding of repentance would radically alter their lives by reshaping their thinking and moral vision. But, if they reject John's message and refuse to repent, they would experience judgment. This is the theme of John's message that ties him, as well as Malachi, to the 'Olivet teaching' of Jesus. Since the Kingdom is near, judgment is near. John makes this clear in a very strong statement directed to the Pharisees and Sadducees - "...You brood of vipers! Who warned you to flee from the wrath to come? Bear fruit in keeping with repentance. And do not presume to say to yourselves, 'We have Abraham as our father,' for I tell you, God is able from these stones to raise up children for Abraham. Even now the axe is laid to the root of the trees. Every tree therefore that does not bear good fruit is cut down and thrown into the fire. "I baptize you with water for repentance, but he who is coming after me is mightier than I, whose sandals I am not worthy to carry. He will baptize you with the Holy Spirit and fire. His winnowing fork is in his hand, and he will clear his threshing floor and gather his wheat into the barn, but the chaff he will burn with unquenchable fire (Matt.3:7-12)."

This warning is not an empty one. The phrase 'the wrath to come' carries the idea of imminence. It is not to be understood as an indefinite future reference. In fact, the axe had already been 'laid to the root of the trees'. The 'axe of judgment' had struck, or was soon to strike. Notice, also, that the 'coming one', the one who would follow John, would baptize with the 'Holy Spirit and fire'. He would inaugurate the 'Messianic Age', which is a New Covenant reference, by baptizing believers with the Holy Spirit (Ezek.36:27). Also, he would bring judgment and separate the 'wheat' from the 'chaff'. This message reflects the prophetic witness of Malachi who said that the Lord would 'suddenly come to his temple' (3:1) and 'draw near to [them] for judgment' (3:5). But, 'before the great and awesome [dreadful] day of the Lord' came, 'Elijah the prophet' (i.e. John the Baptist) would be sent (4:5), and he would call the people to repentance (4:6). If they refused to repent the Lord would 'strike the land [Israel] with a decree of utter destruction' (4:6). The Jewish way of life, including their political structures and religious system, would be destroyed.

John the Baptist was a transitional figure whose arrival marked the beginning of the end of the Jewish Age. He announced the in-breaking of the Messianic Age, the long awaited rule of God.

CHAPTER 4

Redefining the Kingdom

After four hundred years of prophetic silence, John the Baptist arrives on the scene. He comes to announce the soon arrival of Messiah and also, to signal the coming 'great and dreadful day of the Lord' (Malachi 4:5). Once John identifies Jesus as the 'coming one', the promised Messiah, and baptizes him, he shares the historical stage with him for only a short time. He is soon arrested and executed by Herod the Tetrarch.

When Jesus heard that John the Baptist had been arrested, he 'withdrew into Galilee' and settled in the village of Capernaum in the territory of Zebulun and Nephtali. According to Matthew's gospel, this is significant because it set the stage for the fulfillment of a prophecy found in Isaiah chapter nine -

> *"The land of Zebulun and the land of Naphtali, the way of the sea, beyond the Jordan, Galilee of the Gentiles—the people dwelling in darkness have seen a great light, and for those dwelling in the region and shadow of death, on them a light has dawned (Matt.4:15,16)."*

This prophecy of Isaiah clearly said that the northern regions of Israel – Zebulun and Nephtali – would be the first to experience the 'light' [the disclosure] of the Messiah. What Matthew does is use messianic material from the Prophets to support his conviction that Jesus is the expected Messiah and also, to suggest that Gentiles will be included in the Messianic Kingdom. This is seen in the reference to 'Galilee of the Gentiles' (v.15). This Gentile inclusion was unexpected and considered impossible by the majority of the Jews of Jesus' day.

What Jesus does in his public ministry is continue the proclamation of John, announcing the arrival of the Kingdom [the rule] of God. And yet, he strengthens the announcement by adding Old Testament exposition and miraculous manifestations to his pronouncement. His basic announcement is the same as John's - "Repent, for the Kingdom of heaven is at hand" (Matt.4:17). Mark, in his gospel, gives us some additional information - "The time is fulfilled, and the kingdom of God is at hand; repent and believe in the gospel (Mk.1:15)." With the phrase - 'the time is fulfilled' - Mark is making it plain that the season of preparation and messianic expectation was over. The Kingdom of God had arrived embodied in Christ, the long awaited Messiah.

The Messianic Profile

Also, it is important to remember the messianic profile given by John the Baptist - "...He will baptize you with the Holy Spirit and fire. His winnowing fork is in his hand, and he will clear his threshing floor and gather his wheat into the barn, but the chaff he will burn with unquenchable fire (Matt.3:11b, 12)." The first descriptive line underscores the defining feature of the New Covenant; all believers will be brought into the life of Spirit. They will be 'baptized in the Holy Spirit', which is a reference to the Messiah's redemptive work - he is the Savior! The Kingdom of God is essentially tethered to Christ's saving work at Calvary; its underpinnings are spiritual, not political. Also, the arrival of Christ on the historical stage fulfilled Moses' prophecy - "The Lord your God will raise up for you a prophet like me from among you, from your brothers - it is to him you shall listen - (Deut.18:15)." As Moses was the Mediator of the Old Covenant, Jesus is the Mediator of the New. In addition, the Messiah would bring judgment - "...his winnowing fork is in his hand...". He would bring judgment on the old Mosaic system; the religious structures of the Jewish Age [the Old Covenant Age] were passing away.

Now, Jesus' announcement of the Kingdom's arrival is strengthened by some distinguishing features of his public ministry. He engaged in three specific expressions of ministry. First, he taught the people through Old Testament exposition, clarifying the nature and purpose of the Kingdom of God. A good example of this is his 'Sermon on the Mount' (Matt.5-7). He also preached the good news of the Kingdom's 'in-breaking', announcing that God's sovereign purposes in history were finally being realized. And, finally, he healed the sick, dramatically demonstrating the arrival of the Kingdom (Matt.4:23-25). The Kingdom of God had truly arrived, but it was not fully manifested. That will occur with Christ's return at the end of human history. So, presently we live in the 'now' and the 'not yet' tension of the Kingdom.

Redefining the Kingdom

What Jesus actually does is challenge the Jewish expectation and redefine the common Kingdom understanding. The Jews were expecting a dramatic apocalyptic 'in-breaking' of the Kingdom; Jesus taught the Kingdom's progressive unfolding. To support his position he often used agricultural analogies. These provided a vivid point of reference for the people he spoke to. He likened the arrival and development of the Kingdom of God to that of a farmer scattering seed; the seed sprouts and grows. Initially, the Kingdom is almost invisible; it appears to be weak and powerless. It goes unnoticed. It presents itself first as a 'blade', then as an 'ear', and then the "full grain in the ear". The Kingdom has humble beginnings, like that of a mustard seed (the 'smallest of all seeds') which when planted grows and becomes larger than 'all the garden plants'. And when full grown it provides shade and a resting place for the 'birds of the air' (Mk.4:26-32). This certainly wasn't what the Jews were anticipating; this wasn't an apocalypic 'inbreaking'.

Also, the Jews expected the Kingdom to be nationalistic and exclusive. Jesus taught that the Kingdom was inclusive and universal. He claimed to be the 'Good Shepherd' who had "...other sheep that are not of this fold. I must bring them also, and they will listen to my voice. So there will be one flock, one shepherd (Jn.10:16)." You can hear this same understanding in the 'Great Commission' - "Go therefore and make disciples of all nations, baptizing them in the name of the Father and the Son and of the Holy Spirit, (Matt.28:19)." This universal inclusion is exactly what the prophet Daniel had predicted - "And to him [Messiah] was given dominion and glory and a kingdom, that all peoples, nations, and languages should serve him;... (Dan.7:14)." The inclusive and open understanding of the Kingdom, as Jesus announced it to be, was radical and foreign to Jewish ears. Jews were expecting the geopolitical restoration of Israel as a world dominating power led by the Messiah. Just as King David had done in the past, so would the Messiah do. He would liberate them from their enemies, and rule the world from the throne of David in Jerusalem. Jesus understood 'Kingdom-rule' very differently. He said his Kingdom was 'not of this world'(Jn.18:36), and that it was already in the midst of them (Lk.17:21). His Kingdom was spiritual, not geographical and political.

What the Jewish leaders were expecting was the restoration of Kingdom power and prominence to Israel; whereas, Jesus taught that the Kingdom had been taken from them - "Therefore I tell you, the kingdom of God will be taken away from you and given to a people producing its fruits (Matt.21:43)." Luke records a pivotal moment in the Apostle Paul's ministry when he says something similar to the Jews in Antioch in Pisidia - "And Paul and Barnabas spoke out boldly, saying, "It was necessary that the word of God be spoken first to you. Since you thrust it aside and judge yourselves unworthy of eternal life, behold, we are turning to the Gentiles. For so the Lord has commanded us, saying, 'I have made you a light for the Gentiles, that you may bring salvation to the ends of the earth.'" And when the Gentiles heard this, they began rejoicing and glorifying the word of the Lord, and as many as were appointed to eternal life believed (Acts 13:46-48)."

What shaped the Jewish understanding of the Kingdom was secular 'Apocalypicism', not biblical prophecy. The Jews were expecting Messianic deliverance, but instead they would receive judgment, and it was not far off. Jesus spoke to this quite often. When he sent out the Twelve, for example, he said - "Brother will deliver brother over to death, and the father his child, and children will rise against parents and have them put to death, and you will be hated by all for my name's sake. But the one who endures to the end will be saved. When they persecute you in one town, flee to the next, for truly, I say to you, you will not have gone through all the towns of Israel before the Son of Man comes (Matt.10:21-23)."

Later, in Matthew sixteen, Jesus restates this same idea to his disciples when he startles them by saying that some of those listening to him would be alive to witness his coming in judgment on Jerusalem (Matt.16:24-28). Again, in a series of 'woes' addressed to the Pharisees, Jesus made a disturbing prediction that because they persecuted and killed the prophets, judgment would come upon their generation and the Temple would be desolated (Matt.23:36,38). As disturbing as this prediction is, Luke adds details that makes it even more startling - "And when he drew near and saw the city, he wept over it, saying, "Would that you, even you, had known on this day the things that make for peace! But now they are hidden from your eyes. For the days will come upon you, when your enemies will set up a barricade around you and surround you and hem you in on every side and tear you down to the ground, you and your children within you. And they will not leave one stone upon another in you, because you did not know the time of your visitation (Lk.19:41-44)."

This is not a picture of deliverance and restoration to power; it is a description of judgment. Within that generation, Jerusalem and the Temple would be totally destroyed; not one stone would be left on another because they had rejected the Messiah. It appears that the flow of events was moving steadily toward a decisive and horrific judgment event, and this is what the 'Olivet Prophecy' is about.

CHAPTER 5

Prophetic Consummation

S ome of the most remarkable things about biblical prophecy are its continuity and the precision with which it speaks. So, before we turn our attention to the 'Olivet Prophecy' as recorded in Matthew 24, let's give some attention to a prophecy found in Daniel chapter nine. This prophecy is Messianic and speaks precisely to the redemptive work of Christ and the judgment he would bring on Jerusalem. The prophecy is found in Daniel 9:24-27 -

> "Seventy weeks are decreed about your people and your holy city, to finish the transgression, to put an end to sin, and to atone for iniquity, to bring in everlasting righteousness, to seal both vision and prophet, and to anoint a most holy place. Know therefore and understand that from the going out of the word to restore and build Jerusalem to the coming of an anointed one, a prince, there shall be seven weeks. Then for sixty-two weeks it shall be built again with squares and moat, but in a troubled time. And after the sixty-two weeks, an anointed one shall be cut off and shall have nothing. And the people of the prince

*who is to come shall destroy the city and the sanctuary. Its
end shall come with a flood, and to the end there shall be
war. Desolations are decreed. And he shall make a strong
covenant with many for one week, and for half of the week
he shall put an end to sacrifice and offering. And on the
wing of abominations shall come one who makes desolate,
until the decreed end is poured out on the desolator."*

The opening verse of this prophecy (v.24) describes redemption, which
is one aspect of the Messiah's work, and it places this work in a time frame
of 490 years [70x7]. Six statements are made that fall quite naturally into
two groups of three. The first three tell us what the redeeming work of
Christ [the Messiah] will accomplish. First, he will restrict or hinder the
free expression of human sinfulness; he will "finish the transgression".
John, in the Revelation, speaks to this when he says that Satan will be
bound for a thousand years [understood as an extended period of time] and
not allowed to deceive the nations at will (Rev.20:3). This set the stage for
the effective evangelization of the Roman world after Pentecost. The next
statement - "to put an end to sin" - tells us that the offense of sin will be set
aside and removed from God's sight by the Savior's work of propitiation
and expiation. Christ would bear the judgment we deserve and clear away
the offense on our behalf. John speaks of this as well - "In this is love,
not that we have loved God but that he loved us and sent his Son to be
the propitiation for our sins (1Jn.4:10)." The third statement adds to this
redemptive understanding - "to atone for iniquity". Christ, the Messiah,
would establish the judicial basis for our forgiveness by offering himself as
the final atoning sacrifice. No additional sin-offerings will ever be needed!
These three statements speak directly to the redeeming work of Christ, the
Messiah.

Christ's Work as Redeemer

In addition to these statements, there are three more that identify
issues directly related to Christ's work as Redeemer. He would "bring in
everlasting righteousness." In other words, God's righteousness would
be brought into the human situation and completely cover the redeemed
sinner. The Prophet Malachi speaks of this when he describes the 'Great
Day of the Lord' - "But for you who fear my name, the sun of righteousness
shall rise with healing in its wings. You shall go out leaping like calves from

the stall (Mal.4:2)." The God who is righteous and demands righteousness on the part of those who would have fellowship with him, has provided righteousness for those who repent and trust Christ alone for salvation. This is great news! This promise is followed up by this statement - "to seal both vision and prophet". To 'seal up' means to confirm or fulfill. What is promised here is that this prophecy would be fulfilled within the 490 year period set by God's decree. The final statement is "to anoint a most holy place." In the context of this redemptive discussion, Malachi's statement refers to the setting apart of a new dwelling place of God, which is the Church living under the rule of God. The Church is the 'most holy place'. This is certainly compatible with John's description of the Church in its full redeemed splendor as the 'Bride of Christ' and the 'New Jerusalem' in which there is no Temple (Rev. 21).

The balance of the prophecy (vv. 25-27) breaks this prophetic 490 years into two distinct periods of time and identifies the significant events that occur in each of these prophetic seasons. Daniel writes in verse 25 - "Know therefore and understand that from the going out of the word to restore and build Jerusalem to the coming of an anointed one, a prince, there shall be seven weeks. Then for sixty-two weeks it shall be built again with squares and moat, but in a troubled time." Here we have a specific time reference that begins with the King's decree to rebuild Jerusalem and ends with the public presentation of the Messiah ["anointed one"]. The calculation is that 483 years will pass between these two events (7 x 7 = 49 years and 62 x 7 = 434 years which totals to 483 years). This prophecy was fulfilled precisely. The order to rebuild Jerusalem was issued by the Persian King Artaxerxes I in 458 BC, and Christ at his baptism was publicly presented by John the Baptist as the Messiah in 26 AD; exactly 483 years after Artaxerxes' decree. Also, during that time Jerusalem was rebuilt with "squares" and "moat" [or streets and a barrier - a wall] during "a troubled time", just as Daniel prophecied.

The Seventh Week of Daniel's Prophecy

There is a shift of focus in verses 26-27 of Daniel's prophecy. Our attention is drawn to the 'seventh' week: the seven years that follow the Messiah's public disclosure. These verses underscore issues related to the Messiah's redemptive work that are described in verse 24, and they also speak of the coming destruction of Jerusalem - "And after the sixty-two weeks, an anointed one shall be cut off and shall have nothing. And the people of the prince who is to come shall destroy the city and the sanctuary. Its end shall come with a flood, and to the end there shall be war. Desolations are decreed. And he shall make a strong covenant with many for one week, and for half of the week he shall put an end to sacrifice and offering. And on the wing of abominations shall come one who makes desolate, until the decreed end is poured out on the desolator." These are parallel verses that essentially share the same information, like snap-shots of the same subject. For this reason, they need to be considered together. The first thing to notice is that this seven year period is a period of 'covenant confirmation' - "And he [the Messiah, not the Anti-Christ] shall make a strong covenant with many for one week [one seven]...(v.27)." Jesus came announcing and confirming through miraculous signs and wonders the arrival of the Kingdom of God which was founded on the 'New Covenant ' in his blood (Lk.22:20). However, in the middle of this seven year period the Messiah was 'cut off' (v.26); Christ was crucified. But, with his death the redemption described in verse 24 was accomplished, and the Old Covenant Age was brought to an end - "...he [Messiah] shall put an end to sacrifice and offering (v.27)". In other words, the Jewish sacrificial system and all it foreshadowed was fulfilled and brought to a close. The seven year period of 'covenant confirmation' directed to the Jews was actually completed through the Apostolic witness which is understood to be an extension of Christ's ministry (Acts 1:1,2). With the stoning of Stephen in 33 AD the evangelistic focus began to turn to the Gentiles who were more responsive to the gospel (Acts 13:46).

The Final Thing

The final thing that occurs in this seventieth week is the issuing of the divine decree that Jerusalem would be judged and destroyed - "... on the wing of abominations shall come one who makes desolate, until the decreed end is poured out on the desolator (v.27)." Because Jewish leaders rejected Christ as their Messiah, the judgment of Jerusalem was determined and would be carried out before that generation passed from the scene. Daniel describes the judgment of Jerusalem quite vividly - "... the people of the prince [a reference to the armies of Rome used by God as the instrument of judgment] who is to come shall destroy the city and the sanctuary. Its end shall come with a flood, and to the end there shall be war. Desolations are decreed (v.26)." Then add to this the final lines of v.27 - "... Then on a wing of horrors shall a desolator come to bring ruin until a fully determined end comes down on the desolation (Berkeley version)." This is exactly what Jesus had in mind when he spoke to the crowd following him to Golgotha - "Daughters of Jerusalem, do not weep for me, but weep for yourselves and for your children. For behold, the days are coming when they will say, 'Blessed are the barren and the wombs that never bore and the breasts that never nursed!' Then they will begin to say to the mountains, 'Fall on us,' and to the hills, 'Cover us.' For if they do these things when the wood is green, what will happen when it is dry (Lk.23:28-31)?" Horrific judgment was coming, and God was about to bring to a close the Jewish Age. This is what prompted the questions of Christ's disciples that lead to the 'Olivet Prophecy' - "As he sat on the Mount of Olives, the disciples came to him privately, saying, "Tell us, when will these things be, and what will be the sign of your coming and of the end of the age (Matt.24:3)?" In this question the disciples express their grave concern, their confusion, a sense of urgency. They have been expecting political liberation and the rebirth of Israel's 'golden age'. What Jesus is predicting does not sound like liberation and rebirth! It sounds like something dramatically different. Is he predicting the complete disruption of their religious life and even greater national grief? If the temple is destroyed (Matt.24:2) what else could it means? In reality, there are many dark days ahead.

CHAPTER 6

The Olivet Question

I n his public preaching ministry, Jesus is a Prophet in the classic Old Testament sense. He exposes the sin and hypocrisy of the Jewish authorities and calls the people to repentance in the face of the 'in-breaking' of God's rule. If the people do not repent, he warns that judgment is imminent. Jesus' message is clearly prophetic and not apocalyptic, in that he does not offer the comfort and hope of Messianic deliverance which is characteristic of Apocalyptic literature. What he does is restate the judgment message of the 'post Exilic' prophets, particularly the warning of Malachi. Malachi warned that the "great and awesome day of the Lord" (Mal.4:5) was coming, and if they did not repent the Lord would "come and strike the land with a decree of utter destruction (Mal.4:6)."

The closing paragraph of Matthew chapter 23 serves as a transition into the 'Olivet Prophecy' recorded in chapter 24. The discourse is an extension and enlargement on a series of indictments brought by Jesus against the Jewish authorities. The language he uses is strong; he calls them 'serpents', and a 'brood of vipers' (Matt.23:33). He goes on to accuse them of spiritual blindness, human brutality, and an unwillingness to believe; they persecuted and killed the prophets God had sent to them (Matt.23:34,35). His final prediction had to be disturbing and unbelievable - "See, your house [Temple] will be left to you desolate [destroyed, deserted, uninhabitable, forsaken]" (Matt.23:38). And this judgment was not far off, it was imminent (v.36 - "...all these things will come upon this generation"). The only thing that would delay or turn the judgment aside was genuine repentance (v.39). With this said, Jesus left the Temple, never to return to it.

The Disciples' Questions

As Jesus was leaving the Temple, his disciples asked him a number of pressing questions and he made some startling prophetic statements -

> *"Jesus left the temple and was going away, when his disciples came to point out to him the buildings of the temple. But he answered them, "You see all these, do you not? Truly, I say to you, there will not be left here one stone upon another that will not be thrown down." As he sat on the Mount of Olives, the disciples came to him privately, saying, "Tell us, when will these things be, and what will be the sign of your coming [your coming in judgment on apostate Israel] and of the end of the age [the Old Covenant Age] (Matt.24:1-3)?"*

With the prediction of 'desolation' still large in their minds, the disciples drew the Lord's attention to the massive stonework of the Temple. According to Josephus, the first century Jewish historian, the stones were 50 feet long, 24 feet high and 16 feet thick. As they looked at the Temple Jesus asked a rhetorical question, and then made a prediction - "...You see all these, do you not? Truly, I say to you, there will not be left here one stone upon another that will not be thrown down [these stones will be thrown down] (Matt.24:2)." Jesus is referring to this Temple, Herod's Temple, that was still under construction. What he was saying is that Jerusalem and the existing Temple of that time is the subject of the 'Olivet Prophecy'. He was not talking about some reconstructed Temple off in the far future. This question and prediction puts a general 'time-frame' around the prophetic details of the prophecy. This should determine the interpretive approach that should be applied to it.

There is a second set of questions posed by the disciples in verse 3, and this set of questions is focused on three interrelated events. When will the Temple be destroyed? What will signal the coming of Christ in judgment on Jerusalem? And it was understood that if the Temple was destroyed the Old Covenant Age would end. The answer to the 'when' question is given in two statements later in the prophecy - "Truly, I say to you, this generation will not pass away until all these things take place.(v.34)" .... "But concerning that day and hour no one knows, not even the angels of heaven, nor the Son, but the Father only (v.36)." So, a general time-frame is given, 'this generation' (approx. 40 years), but the specific 'day and hour' is only known to the Father. As to the 'what' question regarding the 'sign' of his coming, there is no single indicator; but rather, an unfolding social, political, and religious climate that climaxes with the fall of Jerusalem, the destruction of the Temple, and the end of the 'Age'.

The Close of the Age

It is important that we understand what is meant by the 'close of the age'. This reference is made only by Matthew because he is writing to a Jewish audience. The word used here is not 'cosmos' (κόσμος), translated 'world' in the Authorized Version; rather it is 'aion' (αἰών), translated 'age'. It refers to a period of time, to an era or epoch. So it speaks of a 'time-period' in divine history, an idea that was familiar to the Jews. George Hill, in a lecture entitled 'Predictions Delivered by Jesus' (1847), writes: "Time was divided by the Jews into two great periods, the age of the law and the age of the Messiah. The conclusion of the one was the beginning of the other." [1] The disciples, then, were anticipating the close of one 'Age' and the beginning of another. From the later Apostolic perspective the 'end of the Age' was the end of the exclusive Jewish entitlement to the Covenant promises; the Gentiles were now included as well.

So the Jewish Age was about to be forever ended, not the physical 'world' and human history. This is clearly the understanding presented in the developing theology of the Apostolic period. The author of Hebrews speaks to this in the context of his presentation of Christ as the High Priest of a better covenant - "In speaking of a new covenant, he makes the first one obsolete. And what is becoming obsolete and growing old is ready to vanish away (Heb.8:13)." The reference is made again in chapter 9:24-26 -

> *"For Christ has entered, not into holy places made with hands, which are copies of the true things, but into heaven itself, now to appear in the presence of God on our behalf.*

---

[1] George Hill, 'Predictions Delivered by Jesus', Lectures in Divinity (New York: Robert Carter, 1847), 103-104.

*Nor was it to offer himself repeatedly, as the high priest
enters the holy places every year with blood not his own,
for then he would have had to suffer repeatedly since the
foundation of the world. But as it is, he has appeared once
for all at the end of the ages to put away sin by the sacrifice
of himself."* The Apostle Paul agrees - *"Now these things
happened to them as an example, but they were written
down for our instruction, on whom the end of the ages has
come (1Cor.10:11)."*

Before we can properly work with the details of the 'Olivet Prophecy'
we need to understand that the 'coming' of Christ under discussion here
is associated with the predicted Messianic judgment on Jerusalem and the
Jewish polity which brings the Jewish Age, with the foreshadowing of its
sacrificial system, to an end. And this judgment would occur before that
generation passed away, but no specific date is given. The fact that Jesus said
that "...this generation [approximately 40 years] will not pass away until all
these things take place (Matt. 24:34)", forces us to consider seriously the
destruction of Jerusalem and the Temple in 70 AD by the Romans as the
fulfillment of this prophecy.

Why Treat the 'Olivet Prophecy' Historically?

This understanding of the 'Olivet Prophecy's' fulfillment raises a
companion question - "why?" Why treat the 'Olivet Prophecy' historically
rather than a futuristic reference? First, the historical approach to the
discourse conforms naturally to the Old Testament description of the
Messianic mission. Concisely put, the Messiah would establish a New
Covenant by giving himself as the final sacrifice for sin, fulfilling the Old
Covenant types and foreshadowings. His mission was certainly redemptive
(Ps.22; Isa.53), but he would also bring judgment on the Jewish religious and
political structures of that day. He would put an end to the Jewish sacrificial
system, and literally bring the Old Covenant Age to a close (Dan.9; Mal.3,4).
Also, the historical approach is the 'majority' approach of the early church
fathers and the Protestant Reformers. For example, Eusebius the 4th
century church historian sums up the church Fathers' understanding in
his *Ecclesiastical History* - "All this occurred in this manner, in the second
year of the reign of Vespasian, according to the predictions of our Lord
and Savior Jesus Christ, who by his divine power foresaw all these things

as if already present at the time, who wept and mourned indeed, at the prospect, as the holy evangelists show in their writings" [2]. In addition to the pre-fourth century Church fathers, the historical position is held by Augustine, Calvin, Luther, Matthew Henry, Adam Clarke, John Gerstner, R.C. Sproul and Jay Adams, just to cite a few credible Bible scholars. Third, the historical approach takes the gospel's 'time-texts' seriously. Here is a sampling of these texts - "When they persecute you in one town, flee to the next, for truly, I say to you, you will not have gone through all the towns of Israel before the Son of Man comes (Matt.10:23)"... "Peter turned and saw the disciple whom Jesus loved [John] following them, the one who also had leaned back against him during the supper and had said, "Lord, who is it that is going to betray you?" When Peter saw him, he said to Jesus, "Lord, what about this man?" Jesus said to him, "If it is my will that he remain until I come, what is that to you? You follow me! (Jn.21:20-22)." This was a prophetic statement because Peter was martyred before Jerusalem fell and John lived to see its destruction. And then there is this passage from Matthew 26 - "But Jesus remained silent. And the high priest said to him, "I adjure you by the living God, tell us if you are the Christ, the Son of God." Jesus said to him, "You have said so. But I tell you, from now on you will see the Son of Man seated at the right hand of Power and coming on the clouds of heaven (Matt.26:63,64)." When Jesus said "you will see" he was assuring the high priest that he would witness his coming in judgment on Jerusalem. Jesus made it clear that many of his contemporaries would witness his return; not his return at the end of human history [his second coming], but his coming to bring judgment on Jerusalem.

This understanding of Christ's 'coming' is crucial to a proper understanding of the 'Olivet Prophecy'. To misunderstand can lead to tragic conclusions. Bertrand Russell, in his book *Why I Am Not a Christian*, is a good example of this. He understood the 'time-texts', but misunderstood the nature of Christ's return. He thought that Matthew 24 was about the second coming of Christ at the end of human history, and since it did not occur before Jesus' generation passed from the scene, as Jesus predicted, he concluded that Jesus was a false prophet. He dismissed Jesus and refused to believe. This is the tragic result of a wrong understanding, and it is

---

[2] Eusebius, *Ecclesiastical History*, Book III, chapter 7, p. 93 (Baker House, Grand Rapids, Mich., 1976).'

not restricted to Bertrand Russell. Many others have come to the same conclusion and turned their backs on Christ.

Final Thoughts

One final thought: when we force the 'Olivet Prophecy' to speak only of things yet future, it requires us to speculate about the 'this generation' reference Jesus made. Which generation is 'this generation'? This is a challenging and risky business. In order to redefine the 'this generation' time-texts, an event is needed that would indicate which generation this is. The rebirth of Israel as a nation in 1948 seemed to many to be the event. If it was, Christ should have returned around 1988, given that a generation is approximately forty years. Since Christ did not return in that time-frame it was suggested that the retaking of Jerusalem by Israel in 1967 was the appropriate 'start-point'. But Christ did not return before or in 2007. In addition to this kind of calculating, the Temple needs to be rebuilt, the Jewish sacrificial system needs to be reintroduced and the Old Roman Empire has to re-emerge and assert itself again. None of these speculations have materialized. As a result, these prophetic speculations fuel the flames of unbelief and discredit the gospel. We need to be concerned about this, and rethink our approach to the material we find in the 'Olivet Prophecy'. Is it possible that all the conditions and events Jesus said would take place did occur in the years leading up to 70 AD?

CHAPTER 7

Travail Begins

A s we work our way through the Olivet prophecy, we must remember that this is the record of a private conversation. Matthew says "...the disciples came to him privately (Matt.24:3)." Mark names the particular disciples - "...Peter, James, John and Andrew asked him privately (Mk.13:3)." The reason that this is important to be noted is that, this being the case, when the pronoun 'you' is used it refers primarily to the disciples, and also, at times, it will include the Apostolic church of which they are part. This limits the time-context in which the events described here will occur. These events, then, are soon coming and firmly set in a particular historical context. Here is how Jesus begins to answer the disciples' question regarding the sign of his coming and the close of the age -

> *"See that no one leads you astray. For many will come in my name, saying, 'I am the Christ,' and they will lead many astray. And you will hear of wars and rumors of wars. See that you are not alarmed, for this must take place, but the end is not yet. For nation will rise against nation, and kingdom against kingdom, and there will be famines and earthquakes in various places. All these are but the beginning of the birth pains. "Then they will deliver you up to tribulation and put you to death, and you will be hated*

by all nations for my name's sake. And then many will fall
away and betray one another and hate one another. And
many false prophets will arise and lead many astray. And
because lawlessness will be increased, the love of many
will grow cold. But the one who endures to the end will be
saved. And this gospel of the kingdom will be proclaimed
throughout the whole world as a testimony to all nations,
and then the end will come (vv.4-14)."

Jesus begins to answer the disciples' 'what' question by describing the general social, political, and religious climate that will set the stage for his coming. He begins with an admonition to stay alert and watch out for deceptions and those who would attempt to lead them into error and wrong thinking. Apparently, they were entering into challenging times. What will protect them from deception and wrong-headed religious understandings? The teaching of Jesus! This is why he is about to say what he says. This idea is repeated in v.25 - "See [understand], I have told you beforehand." The inference is that they will witness these events. Also, the urgency of his warning would suggest that the disciples and their generation is the generation that would see these things unfold; if not, it is an empty admonition.

General Signs

Now, in vv.5-8, Jesus gives them some general 'signs' that have strong social, political, and religious implications. These contribute to creating an environment that is filled with conflict, hardship, anxiety, and heightened 'apocalyptic' expectations. There will be the appearance of a significant number of false Christs [Messiahs], racial and political conflict is going to intensify, and famine and earthquakes will create great human suffering. What does the historical record say about the activities of false Messiahs [deliverers] in the period of 30-70 AD? There are three mentioned in the book of Acts: Theudas (5:35,36), Simon Magus (8:9,10) and a Jewish insurrectionist from Egypt (21:37,38). These men are mentioned in secular sources as well. Josephus, a first century priest and historian, writes this about Theudas - "Now it came to pass, that while Fadus was procurator of Judea [45AD], that a certain magician, whose name was Theudas, persuaded a great part of the people to take their effects with them, and follow him to the river Jordan; for he told them he was a prophet, and that he would, by his own command, divide the river, and afford them an easy passage over it; and many were deluded by his words."[1] Eusebius, a Christian historian of the early 4th century, mentions Simon Magus in his *Ecclesiastical History* - "But Simon had become so celebrated at that time, and had such influence with those that were deceived by his impostures, that they considered him the great power of God. This same Simon, also, astonished at the extraordinary miracles performed by Philip through the power of God, artfully assumed, and even pretended faith in Christ, so far as to be baptized;..."[2] The Apostle Paul was thought to be the the the Egyptian insurrectionist who had "stirred up a revolt" and led four thousand "men of the Assassins" into the wilderness (Acts 21:37,38). Josephus describes this man's activities in his record of the Jewish wars - "But there was an Egyptian false prophet that did the Jews more mischief than the former; for he was a cheat, and pretended to be a prophet also, and got together thirty thousand men that were deluded by him; these he led round about from the wilderness to the mount which is called the Mount of Olives, and was ready to break into Jerusalem by force from that place; and if he could but once conquer the Roman garrison and the people, he intended to domineer over them by the assistance of those guards of his who were to break into the city with him; but Felix [Procurator in Judea, 53-60 AD] prevented his attempt, and met him with his Roman soldiers, while all the people assisted him in his attack upon him, insomuch that when it came to a battle, the Egyptian ran away with a few others, while the greatest part of those that were with him were either destroyed or taken alive; but the rest of the multitude were dispersed every one to their own homes, and there concealed themselves."[3] Josephus, also, summarizes conditions under Felix - "Now, as for the affairs of the Jews, they grew worse and worse continually; for the country was again filled with robbers and impostors [false Messiahs], who deluded the multitude. Yet did Felix catch and put to death many of those impostors every day, together with the robbers."[4]

In addition to these false Messiahs there would be increasing racial

[1] Josephus, *Antiquities of the Jews*, Book XX, chapter 5.1, p. 418 (Kregel Publications, Grand Rapids, MI 1981)

[2] Eusebius, *Ecclesiastical History*, Book II, chapter 1, p. 50 (Baker Book House, Grand Rapids, MI 1976)

[3] Josephus, *Wars of the Jews*, Book II, chapter 13.5, p. 483 (Kregel Publications, Grand Rapids, MI 1981)

[4] Josephus, *Antiquities of the Jews*, Book XX, chapter 8.5, p. 421

and political conflict. Jesus said there would be 'wars and rumors of war' (v.6) and nation would rise against nation and 'kingdom [basilia – authority structures] against kingdom' (v.7). It was true. The period was filled with racial conflict and political intrigue. Much of this was civil in nature, and it fragmented the Jewish community. Alexander Keith, a 19th century minister in the Church of Scotland, writes - "The Jews resisted the erection of the statue of Caligula in the temple; and such was the dread of Roman resentment, that the fields remained uncultivated. At Caesarea, the Jews and Syrians contended for the mastery of the city. Twenty thousand of the former were put to death and the rest were expelled. Every city in Syria was then divided into two armies and multitudes were slaughtered. Alexandria and Damascus presented a similar scene of bloodshed. About fifty thousand of the Jews fell in the former, and ten thousand in the latter. The Jewish nation rebelled against the Romans; Italy was convulsed with contentions for the empire; and, as a proof of the troublous and warlike character of the period, within the brief space of two years, four emperors, Nero, Galba, Otho, and Vitellius, suffered death."[5]

Tacitus, in his Annals, describes the period as follows - "disturbances in Germany, commotions in Africa, commotions in Thrace, insurrections in Gaul, intrigues among the Parthians, war in Britain and war in Armenia."[6] There was war and conflict from one end of the Roman Empire to the other.

Then, add natural disasters to this racial and political unrest. Jesus went on to say - "...there will be famines and earthquakes in various places (v.7)". In Acts eleven, Luke tells of a prophet named Agabus who predicted an empire wide famine (Acts 11:27,28). This prophecy was fulfilled in 45 AD during the reign of Claudius. But famine was not limited to Judea; it occurred at different times in other regions of the empire. Tacitus, in his Annals, describes the famine of 51 AD in Rome - "This year witnessed many prodigies [signs or omens]....[including] repeated earthquakes... Further portents were seen in a shortage of corn, resulting in famine...It was established that there was no more than fifteen days' supply of food in the city [of Rome]. Only heaven's special favor and a mild winter prevented

---

[5] Alexander Keith, The Evidence of the Truth of the Christian Religion Derived from the Literal Fulfillment of Prophecy Particularly as Illustrated by the History of the Jews, pp. 59-60 (Philadelphia, PA: Presbyterian Board of Publication, n.d.)

[6] Tacitus, Annals of Imperial Rome, quote taken from Last Days Madness, Gary DeMar, chapter 3, p. 53, (American Vision Inc., Atlanta, Georgia, 1997)

catastrophe."[7] During the siege of Jerusalem from 66-70 AD, famine increased the horrors in the city. Josephus described the conditions - "Then did the famine widen its progress, and devoured the people by whole houses and families; the upper rooms were full of women and children that were dying by famine; and the lanes of the city were full of the dead bodies of the aged; the children also and the young men wandered about the marketplaces like shadows, all swelled with the famine, and fell down dead wheresoever their misery seized them."[8] Jesus also said that there would be "earthquakes in various places", and there were. In Acts chapter sixteen, Luke mentions a "great [violent] earthquake" (v.26) that shook the prison in Philippi, leading to the release of Paul and Silas. J.Marcellus Kik, in his book, *An Eschatology of Victory*, provides additional information - "And as to earthquakes, many are mentioned by writers during a period just previous to 70 AD. There were earthquakes in Crete, Smyrna, Miletus, Chios, Samos, Laodicea, Hierapolis, Colosse, Campania, Rome and Judea. It is interesting to note that the city of Pompeii was much damaged by an earthquake occurring on February 5, 63 AD."[9] Edward Plumptre, an English divine and scholar, writes in his commentary on Matthew's gospel - "Perhaps no period in the world's history has ever been so marked by these convulsions as that which intervenes between the Crucifixion and the destruction of Jerusalem."[10] These destructive events were broad-based, affecting the entire Roman Empire. And Jesus said that "all these are but the beginning of the birth pains (v.8)."

Personalized Hardships

There was great persecution coming and many defections from the faith. Others would be couragous and martyred for their unwavering dovotion to Christ (Matt.24:9-13). The book of Acts documents this Christian persecution. Persecutions are mentioned in chapters 4,7,8,12,16,18,24, and 25. Christians, and particularly the Apostles, were "hated by all nations"

[7] Tacitus, *Annals of Imperial Rome*, trans. Michael Grant (London: Penguin Books, 1989), p. 271

[8] Josephus, *Wars of the Jews*, Book V, chapter 12.3, p. 568

[9] J. Marcellus Kik, *An Eschatology of Victory*, chapter 5, p. 93 (Presbyterian and Reformed Publishing Co., Phillipsburg, N.J., 1971)

[10] Edward Hayes Plumptre, *The Gospel According to St. Matthew*, Ellicott's Commentary on the Whole Bible, ed. Charles John Ellicott, 8 vols. (London: Cassell and Company, 1897), 6:146

['ethnos'-peoples]; they were hated by both Jews and Gentiles. After the burning of Rome in 64-65 AD, the persecution of Christians was State-sponsored for the first time. Nero, in an effort to deflect accusations of his involvement in the city's burning, accused the Christians of being responsible. Tertullian, a second-century church father, in his work *The Apology*, says that the people were executed for simply bearing the name Christian - "There was war against the very name of Christ."[11] In connection with this persecution Jesus said that "...many will fall away and betray one another...(v.10)." The Apostle Paul mentions this several times in his second letter to Timothy - "You are aware that all who are in Asia turned away from me...(2Tim.1:15)", "For Demas, in love with this present world, has deserted me...(2Tim.4:10)", "At my first defense no one came to stand by me, but all deserted me...(2Tim.4:16)." This falling away was the result of persecution and the influence of false prophets. False prophets are mentioned throughout the New Testament text (2Cor.11:13, 2Tim.2:16-18, 2Pet.2:1, 1Jn.2:18-19, 4:1). Thomas Newton, in his *Dissertations on the Prophecies* (1754), summarizes this matter quite well - "...who can hear St. Paul complaining at Rome that "at his first answer no man stood with him, but all men forsook him" (2Tim.4:16); who can hear the divine author of the Epistle to the Hebrews, exhorting them "not to forsake the assembling of themselves together, as the manner of some is" (10:25); and not conclude the event to have sufficiently justified our Saviour's prediction?"[12] Persecution and desertion would come and did come.

And yet, with these predicted hardships and desertions Jesus, adds a word of encouragement - "But the one who endures to the end will be saved (v.13)." What end? The context determines it. It is 'the end' of the Old Covenant Age, signaled by the destruction of Jerusalem and the Temple by the Romans. The faithful ones would be spared the horrific suffering and death that was about to overtake Jerusalem. In his work, *The New Testament for English Readers* (1886), Henry Alford writes - "The primary meaning of this seems to be, that whosoever remained faithful till the destruction of Jerusalem, should be preserved from it. No Christians, that

---

[11] Tertullian, *The Apology*, *The Ante-Nicene Fathers*, eds. Alexander Roberts and John Donaldson, vol. 3, chapter 2, pp. 18-20 (Eerdmans, Grand Rapids, MI [1885] 1986)

[12] Thomas Newton, *Dissertations on the Prophecies, Which Have Remarkably Been Fulfilled, and at this Time are Fulfilling in the World*, pp. 340-41 (London: J.F. Dove, 1754)

we know of, perished in the siege or after it."[13] Eusebius tells us how this happened - "The whole body, however, of the church at Jerusalem, having been commanded by a divine revelation, given to men of approved piety there before the war, removed from the city, and dwelt at a certain town beyond the Jordan, called Pella. Here, those that believed in Christ, having removed from Jerusalem, as if holy men had entirely abandoned the royal city itself, and the whole land of Judea; the divine justice, for their crimes against Christ and his apostles, finally overtook them, totally destroying the whole generation of these evildoers from the earth."[14] Josephus provides more detail by telling us that the Roman General Cestius Gallus from Syria was the first to surround Jerusalem with his army. But he unexpectedly withdrew, which gave the Christians in the city opportunity to leave.[15] Jesus had forewarned them -

> *"But when you see Jerusalem surrounded by armies, then know that its desolation has come near. Then let those who are in Judea flee to the mountains, and let those who are inside the city depart, and let not those who are out in the country enter it, for these are days of vengeance, to fulfill all that is written (Lk.21:20-22)."*

The Final Indicator

This brings us to the final indicator that judgment was soon coming - "And this gospel of the kingdom will be proclaimed throughout the whole world as a testimony to all nations, and then the end will come (Matt.24:14)." Jesus speaks very plainly that before judgment comes upon Jerusalem a gospel witness will be given to the 'whole world'. The key to understanding this verse is to understand what is meant by the 'whole world' reference. The Greek word translated 'world' is 'oikoumene' (οἰκουμένη), not 'cosmos' (κόσμος). It refers not to the globe or planet, but to the inhabited world. More precisely, it speaks of people unified by a set of cultural norms. So here, it refers to the Roman Empire which was unified by Hellenistic [Greek] culture. The same word, 'oikoumene', is used in Luke 2:1 clearly in reference to the Roman Empire - "In those days a decree went out from

---

[13] Henry Alford, *The New Testament for English Readers*, p. 164 (Moody Press, [1886] n.d., Chicago, IL)

[14] Eusebius, *Ecclesiastical History*, Book III, chapter 5, p.86

[15] Josephus, *Wars of the Jews*, Book II, chapter 19.7, p. 496

Caesar Augustus that all the world [oikoumene] should be registered."
Caesar Augustus ruled over the Roman world, not the entire inhabited
earth. 'Oikoumene' is used throughout the New Testament as a political
reference to the Roman Empire. We find the same useage of the word in
Acts 11:28 - "And one of them named Agabus stood up and foretold by the
Spirit that there would be a great famine over all the world ['oikoumene'-
the entire Roman Empire] (this took place in the days of Claudius)". So
according to Jesus, the entire Roman world and all the 'nations', or ethnic
groups within the Empire would receive a gospel witness before he came
in judgment on Jerusalem. Not only would the Jews be evangelized; the
gospel would also be preached to the Gentiles throughout the Empire.
The question then is, was the gospel of the Kingdom preached in every
corner of the Roman Empire before 70 AD? Yes. For example, the Apostle
Paul in just ten years (47-57 AD) had evangelized four Roman provinces –
Asia, Galatia, Achaia, and Macedonia. And his intention was to continue
traveling west into Spain. Philip Doddridge, in his volume, *The Family
Expositor*, gives a summary of the historical record - "It appears, from the
most credible records, that the gospel was preached in Idumea, Syria, and
Mesopotamia, by Jude; in Egypt, Marmorica, Mauritania, and other parts
of Africa, by Mark, Simon, and Jude; in Ethiopia, by Candace's Eunuch and
Matthias; in Pontus, Galatia, and the neighbouring parts of Asia, by Peter;
in territories of the seven Asiatic churches, by John; in Parthia, by Matthew;
in Scythia, by Philip and Andrew; in the northern and western parts of
Asia, by Bartholomew; in Persia, by Simon and Jude; in Media, Carmanea,
and several eastern parts, by Thomas; through the vast tract from Jerusalem
round about unto Illyricum, by Paul, as also in Italy, and probably in Spain,
Gaul, and Britain; in most of which places Christian churches were planted,
in less than thirty years after the death of Christ, which was before the
destruction of Jerusalem."[16] This passage in the 'Olivet Discourse' is a
remarkable example of fulfilled biblical prophecy! It should strengthen our
faith and deepen our confidence in the authority of Scripture.

---

[16] Philip Doddridge, *The Family Expositor*, 6 vols., 2:365 (Charlestown, MA: S. Etheridge,
1807)

CHAPTER 8

Travail Intensifies

The prophetic picture painted by Jesus in the opening section of his discourse (Matt. 24:4-14) describes a season which is about to unfold that is marked by deception, ethnic and political conflict, natural disasters, persecution, and defections from the Faith. And yet, the 'gospel of the Kingdom' will be preached throughout the entire Roman world before the end comes. According to the primary historical sources of the period – Josephus, Tacitus, the New Testament record and later, Eusibeus – all of this occurred between 33-70 A.D. These events are simply early features of a gathering storm of judgment that is about to break over Jerusalem.

Now this is not the first time Jesus gave warnings of coming judgment. He had been warning Jewish leadership throughout his public ministry. But the theme becomes more prominent during the closing months of his ministry. He speaks plainly on some occasions, and more muted and less direct on others. There are two examples of this that will serve as a good preface to the next section of the Discourse -

> "And when he drew near and saw the city, he wept over it, saying, "Would that you, even you, had known on this day the things that make for peace! But now they are hidden from your eyes. For the days will come upon you, when your enemies will set up a barricade around you

and surround you and hem you in on every side and tear
you down to the ground, you and your children within
you. And they will not leave one stone upon another in
you, because you did not know the time of your visitation
(Lk.19:41-44)."

The same theme is presented in a parable Jesus tells of a King who prepared a wedding feast for his son and issued an invitation to his people, but they refused to come. They dismissed the invitation and even killed the King's servants who called them to attend the feast. The last line of the parable is chilling and prophetic - "The king was angry and destroyed those murderers and burned their city (Matt.22:7)."

With these forewarnings already in place, Jesus sounds the alarm again -

"So when you see the abomination of desolation spoken of
by the prophet Daniel, standing in the holy place (let the
reader understand), then let those who are in Judea flee
to the mountains. Let the one who is on the housetop not
go down to take what is in his house, and let the one who
is in the field not turn back to take his cloak. And alas for
women who are pregnant and for those who are nursing
infants in those days! Pray that your flight may not be
in winter or on a Sabbath. For then there will be great
tribulation, such as has not been from the beginning of the
world until now, no, and never will be. And if those days
had not been cut short, no human being would be saved.
But for the sake of the elect those days will be cut short.
Then if anyone says to you, 'Look, here is the Christ!' or
'There he is!' do not believe it. For false christs and false
prophets will arise and perform great signs and wonders,
so as to lead astray, if possible, even the elect. See, I have
told you beforehand. So, if they say to you, 'Look, he is in
the wilderness,' do not go out. If they say, 'Look, he is in the
inner rooms,' do not believe it. For as the lightning comes
from the east and shines as far as the west, so will be the
coming of the Son of Man. Wherever the corpse is, there
the vultures will gather (Matt.24:15-28)."

Crucial Signs to Look For

This section of the Olivet Prophecy opens with Jesus giving a crucial sign to look for, a sign that would signal the intensifying of the conflict, and also, a brief opportunity to leave the city. The warning is clear and the instruction is urgent - "So when you see the abomination of desolation spoken of by the prophet Daniel, standing in the holy place (let the reader understand), then let those who are in Judea flee to the mountains (vv.15,16)." As Jesus indicated, the reference to "the abomination of desolation [destruction]" is found only in the Old Testament book of Daniel. It appears three times. It appears in Daniel chapters nine, eleven and twelve. In chapters eleven and twelve it refers to the desecration of the Temple by the Selucid King Antiochus Epiphanes in 168 B.C. The third reference, in chapter nine, is in a Messianic context. It speaks of the destruction of Jerusalem and the Temple by the Romans in 70 A.D. The Roman army was considered an abomination as it laid siege to the sacred city and ultimately destroyed it. Luke, in his gospel, makes it clear that this is the meaning of the reference to 'the abomination of desolation' when he writes - "But when you see Jerusalem surrounded by armies, then know that its desolation has come near. Then let those who are in Judea flee to the mountains, and let those who are inside the city depart, and let not those who are out in the country enter it,...(Lk.21:20,21)." The historian, John Forster, writes - "The representations of Caesar, and of the eagle, on the Roman standards were worshiped by the soldiers of that nation, and thus were, in Hebrew phraseology, 'an abomination'. - With equal propriety is their army described by the word 'desolation'. They plundered and devastated without mercy, and, to use the indignant expression of a hostile chieftain, "Where they have made a desert, they call peace" (Speech of Galgacus, Tacitus; Life of Agricola 30). - They planted their standards before Jerusalem, several furlongs of land around which were accounted holy. The Temple was more particularly called 'the holy place' (Acts 6:13); and on the capture of the city, this prediction was fulfilled to the letter; for the Romans brought 'the Eagles' into the Temple and sacrificed to them there. Out of respect to Jewish scruples, they had always before been left at Cesarea by the Roman Governors."[1] In addition to the sacrilege of the Romans the Jewish Zealots, with their Idumean allies, desecrated the Temple by turning it into a fortress. Josephus writes that the Zealots "went over all the buildings, and the

---

[1] John Forster, *The Gospel-Narrative*, (London: John W. Parker, 1847) (i.e. Josephus, *Wars of the Jews*, 6:6:1)

Temple itself, and fell upon the priests, and those that were about the sacred offices."[2] They killed six thousand temple guards in the Temple itself, and went throughout the city raping, torturing, robbing, and killing the more moderate members of the population.

In the midst of this carnage, the disciples and those first exposed to the gospel narratives were told to leave the city quickly when they witnessed these abominations and saw the approaching Roman army. Remember that Cestius Gallus, the Roman General from Syria, had withdrawn his army from Jerusalem in the Fall of 66 AD and most of the Christians fled the city to Pella in Decopolis. But Titus and his army arrived and encircled the city in the spring of 67 AD. Titus constructed a wall and 'battle works' around Jerusalem in just three days. It was urgent that those Christians still in the city leave quickly. This is the message of verses 16-20 - "then let those who are in Judea flee to the mountains. Let the one who is on the housetop not go down to take what is in his house, and let the one who is in the field not turn back to take his cloak. And alas for women who are pregnant and for those who are nursing infants in those days! Pray that your flight may not be in winter or on a Sabbath." It is important that we notice that Sabbath law was still being enforced, indicating a particular time context. Also, it is important to remember that the most offensive abomination had been committed by the Jewish authorities themselves. They had rejected the Messiah and continued to practice the sacrificial system that Christ, the 'lamb of God', had brought to an end at Calvary. J. Marcellus Kik, in an article entitled, 'Abomination of Desolation' writes - "the real cause for the desolation was found in the spiritual fornication of the Jews, especially their rejection of the Messiah."[3]

Then we are told why such urgency is attached to the instruction to leave Jerusalem - " For then there will be great tribulation, such as has not been from the beginning of the world until now, no, and never will be. And if those days had not been cut short, no human being would be saved. But for the sake of the elect those days will be cut short (vv.21,22)". Once Jerusalem was surrounded by armies a season of 'great tribulation' would begin. It would be a time of unthinkable horror. Jesus said it would be a

---

[2] Josephus, *Wars of the Jews*, Book V, chapter 1. 3, p. 547 (Kregel Publications, Grand Rapids, MI 1981)

[3] J. Marcells Kik, 'Abomination of Desolation', *The Encyclopedia of Christianity*, ed. Edwin H. Palmer, 4 vols. (Wilmington, DE: The National Association of Christian Education, 1964), 1:19

time of tribulation "such as has not been from the beginning of the world until now, no, and never will be." This is an example of Jewish hyperbole or what R.H. Charles calls "a stock eschatological expression" used to underscore the severity and horror of the event. An example of this kind of hyperbole is found in Ezekiel 5:8-11, a prophecy fulfilled by the Babylonian siege on Jerusalem in 587 B.C. -

> *"therefore thus says the Lord GOD: Behold, I, even I, am against you. And I will execute judgments in your midst in the sight of the nations. And because of all your abominations I will do with you what I have not yet done, and the like of which I will never do again. Therefore fathers shall eat their sons in your midst, and sons shall eat their fathers. And I will execute judgments on you, and any of you who survive I will scatter to all the winds. Therefore, as I live, declares the Lord GOD, surely, because you have defiled my sanctuary with all your detestable things and with all your abominations, therefore I will withdraw. My eye will not spare, and I will have no pity."*

A Tragic Situation

Here is the situation faced by the people in Jerusalem in 67 A.D. Because of the 'Feast of Unleaven Bread', the population of the city had swelled to approximately 2.7 million. There was civil disorder in the city, and the Roman General Titus intended to exploit it. Titus' army had surrounded the city; escape was impossible. The stage was set for a great horror! Emma Weston gives this description of events in Jerusalem during the siege based on the record of Josephus (*Wars of the Jews*, books 2-6) - "The warring Jewish factions that were holed up in Jerusalem, raided and murdered day and night and no one opposed them. The citizens were so cowed and fearful they seemed to have lost heart to resist. The worst brigands made a fortress of the Temple and defiled it with no regard for its sacred purpose for God. The Romans had never entered the holy place but gave due respect. Now, these Jews, worse than the heathen, were getting drunk in the Temple. The High Priest armed 6,000 men to guard the entrances to pen them in, but these were all destroyed by the insurgents."[4] "There was no grain to

---

[4] Charles G. Weston, *The Weston Annotated Apostolic Bible*, part I, p. 253

be found in the city so people who looked healthy were deemed to have food. Their houses were broken into and they were mistreated for having food and not sharing it, or tormented if none was found. Starving persons traded valuables for a measure of grain, if some was found, shut themselves in their houses, ate of it unground, or some baked it....Women snatched food from husbands or out of the mouths of the babies that were dying in their arms."[5] "The rebels broke into houses and took food from people's jaws. They beat old men grasping food and dragged women by the hair if they tried to conceal food and dashed babies to the ground. They invented unspeakable methods of torment to use on people to make them admit the location of a loaf of bread or a handful of meal....No city, from the beginning of time, ever suffered such miseries and bred a generation more fruitful in wickedness."[6] "With exits closed, all hope of escape was cut off from the Jews. Famine devoured family after family. The flat roofs were full of women and children in final stages of starvation. Lanes were full of corpses. Being sick themselves, no one had strength to bury the dead. Deep silence seized upon the city. No lamentation was heard. The stench was intolerable. Some dead were piled in public buildings and the doors locked. They said 115,830 bodies of the poor were thrown out through one gate. Many others were cast down from the walls. How many others there were, no one knew. When Titus saw these piles of putrefying carcasses, he raised his hands to heaven and called on God to witness, that this was not his doing."[7] "The Romans set fire to outlying areas and demolished the walls to the ground, with not one stone left upon another. The Temple buildings were razed to the very foundations, and the site of the city was rendered utterly desolate, a dwelling place for jackals, save where the Tenth Legion was left, encamped under the shelter of part of the Western wall, to guard the ruins and prevent all attempts at restoration. And so it lay from September A.D. 70 to the year A.D. 122."[8] Dr. D.A. Carson also comments on the suffering in Jerusalem during the Roman siege - "The savagery, slaughter, disease, and famine (mothers eating their own children) were monstrous (cf. Jos. War V, 424-38 [x. 2-3]), 'unequaled from the beginning of the world until now,' and, according to Jesus, 'never to be equaled again.' There have been greater numbers of deaths – six million in the Nazi death

[5] Ibid., p. 258
[6] Ibid., p. 258
[7] Ibid., p. 259
[8] Ibid., p. 263

camps, mostly Jews, and an estimated twenty million under Stalin – but never so high a percentage of a great city's population so thoroughly and painfully exterminated and enslaved as during the Fall of Jerusalem."[9]

In light of the historical record, how could anyone survive? Survival was possible only by the intervention of God's grace in the midst of judgment, shortening the days. For the Christians, they were forewarned and escaped. And for the general population, the days were also shortened. Adam Clarke comments on this in his commentary on Matthew 24:22 – "The besieged themselves helped to shorten those days by their divisions and mutual slaughters; and by fatally deserting their strong holds, where they never could have been subdued, but by famine alone. So well fortified was Jerusalem, and so well provided to stand a siege, that the enemy without could not have prevailed, had it not been for the factions and seditions within. When Titus was viewing the fortifications after the taking of the city, he could not help ascribing his success to God. 'We have fought,' said he, 'with God on our side; and it is God who pulled the Jews out of these strongholds: for what could machines or the hands of men avail against such towers as these?" (War, b. vi. c. 9.) [10] What Jesus predicted did come true!

False Messiahs & False Prophets

This section of the Discourse ends with a second warning that false Messiahs and false prophets would be very active as the siege intensified. Some would even perform signs and miracles. For example, according to St. Jerome, a false prophet by the name of Barcocab pretended to vomit flames of fire.[11] What these false prophets shared in common was their message...'deliverance is imminent because the Messiah has arrived'. They claimed that he was in the desert or in a secret chamber. Jesus said, 'do not believe it' (Matt.24:26). Josephus records this – "A false prophet was the occasion of these people's destruction, who had made a public proclamation in the city that very day, that God commanded them to get upon the temple, and that there they should receive miraculous signs of their deliverance. Now, there was then a great number of false prophets suborned by the tyrants to impose upon the people, who denounced this to them, that they

[9] D.A. Carson, *Expositor's Bible Commentary*, (Zondervan Publishing House, Grand Rapids, MI, 1984) p.501
[10] Adam Clarke, *Adam Clarke's Commentary on Matthew 24:22*, (1837)
[11] Ibid., Matt. 24:23

should wait for deliverance from God..."[12] But, Jesus said his coming in judgment would be very public and dramatic, like lightning flashing from the east to the west (Matt.24:27). 'Lightning' is a common apocalyptic image of divine judgment often used by the Old Testament prophets (i.e. Ezek.21:15,28; Zech.9:14). The Roman army had become the instrument of divine judgment in the hands of the 'Son of Man'. Verse 28 indicates that the vultures would come to devour the carcasses. This is a metaphorical statement. Vultures sense impending death. Titus anticipated the internal collapse of Jerusalem.

The pressing question is – was this siege an expression of divine judgment? Josephus, the Jewish historian, was convinced that it was - "I believe that, had the Romans delayed their punishment of these villains, the city would have been swallowed up by the earth, or overwhelmed with a flood, or, like Sodom, consumed with fire from heaven. For the generation which was in it was far more ungodly than the men on whom these punishments had in former times fallen. By their madness the whole nation came to be ruined."[13] The Olivet Prophecy of Jesus, given forty years prior, had been fulfilled!

---

[12] Josephus, *Wars of the Jews*, Book VI, chapter 5.1, p. 582 (Kregel Publications, Grand Rapids, MI 1981)

[13] Ibid., Book V, chapter 13.6, p. 570

CHAPTER 9

Travail Culminates

Throughout the history of the church there have been speculations regarding the return of Christ and the end of the world. Every generation has had its predictions that have proven to be false. And these false predictions have damaged the faith of many believers and discredited our Christian witness. Many, if not all, of these predictions appeal to the material found in the Olivet Prophecy, particularly the material found in verses 29-35 of Matthew 24 -

> *"Immediately after the tribulation of those days the sun will be darkened, and the moon will not give its light, and the stars will fall from heaven, and the powers of the heavens will be shaken. Then will appear in heaven the sign of the Son of Man, and then all the tribes of the earth will mourn, and they will see the Son of Man coming on the clouds of heaven with power and great glory. And he will send out his angels with a loud trumpet call, and they will gather his elect from the four winds, from one end of heaven to the other. "From the fig tree learn its lesson: as soon as its branch becomes tender and puts out its leaves, you know that summer is near. So also, when you see all these things, you know that he is near, at the very gates.*

Truly, I say to you, this generation will not pass away until
all these things take place. Heaven and earth will pass
away, but my words will not pass away."

A Fundamental Question

This passage raises a fundamental question: are the images presented here to be understood literally or are they prophetic metaphors? Is Jesus using well established apocalyptic language that communicates truth metaphorically [figuratively] rather than literally? Or is he predicting an event that will disrupt the Cosmos [the sun and moon going dark and stars falling from the sky] and bring about the end of human history? The answer to these questions will determine the direction the on-going conversation will take. If Jesus is describing events surrounding his literal, physical return, which we as decided Christians anticipate, we are forced to ignore or redefine verse 34 which is a clear 'time text' - "Truly, I say to you, this generation will not pass away until all these things take place." If Jesus was saying that his bodily second coming would occur before that generation [the generation that witnessed his incarnation] passed from the scene, then we are forced to conclude that Jesus was a false prophet. This was a point of argument in Bertrand Russell's lecture 'Why I Am Not a Christian'.[1] However, if we respect the 'time text', we must, then, treat the language metaphorically and strive to understand its symbolism biblically. We are required to let the 'time text' and the disciples' questions (v.3) dictate our approach to the passage. This is a symbolic literary form that describes a profoundly significant event in divine history.

The language Jesus uses is vivid and powerful - "Immediately after the tribulation of those days the sun will be darkened, and the moon will not give its light, and the stars will fall from heaven, and the powers of the heavens will be shaken (v.29)." Jesus says that without delay after the distress of those days, when Jerusalem and the Temple come under siege and are destroyed, a startling, cosmic disruption would occur. The sun and moon would go dark, the stars would fall from the sky and the heavenly bodies would be shaken. How should we understand this description? This is apocalyptic imagery and judgment language, which is a classic literary form found in Old Testament prophecy. Dr. Colin Brown, in an

---

[1] Bertrand Russell, Lecture: 'Why I Am Not a Christian', presented at the Battersea Town Hall, 'South London Branch of the National Secular Society, England (Mar.6,1927)

article entitled 'Generation', writes the following - "The imagery of cosmic phenomena is used in the Old Testament to describe this-worldly events and, in particular, historical acts of judgment.".…"The cosmic imagery draws attention to the divine dimension of the event in which the judgment of God is enacted.".… "In view of this, Mark 13:24-30 may be interpreted as a prophecy of judgment on Israel in which the Son of man will be vindicated. Such a judgment took place with the destruction of Jerusalem, the desecration of the Temple and the scattering of Israel all of which happened within the lifetime of 'this generation.' The disintegration of Israel as the people of God coincides with the inauguration of the kingdom of the Son of man. Such an interpretation fits the preceding discourse and the introductory remarks of the disciples."[2] What we have here is judgment language commonly used in the Old Testament. For example, we see it in Isaiah's prophecy against Babylon -

> *"Behold, the day of the LORD comes, cruel, with wrath and fierce anger, to make the land a desolation and to destroy its sinners from it. For the stars of the heavens and their constellations will not give their light; the sun will be dark at its rising, and the moon will not shed its light. I will punish the world for its evil, and the wicked for their iniquity; I will put an end to the pomp of the arrogant, and lay low the pompous pride of the ruthless (Isa.13:9-11)."*

This same kind of language is used by Ezekiel when he prophesied judgment on Egypt -

> *"When I blot you out, I will cover the heavens and make their stars dark; I will cover the sun with a cloud, and the moon shall not give its light. All the bright lights of heaven will I make dark over you, and put darkness on your land, declares the Lord God (Ezek.32:7,8)."*

Isaiah prophesying judgment on Edom -

---

[2] Colin Brown, 'Generation', *The International Dictionary of New Testament Theology*, 3 vols. (Grand Rapids, MI: Zondervan, 1976), 2:38

*"All the hosts [stars] of heaven shall rot away [be dissolved],
and the skies roll up like a scroll. All their [starry] host
shall fall,...(Isa.34:4)".*

Because Jesus is a prophet in the Old Testament sense he uses the same
imagery and judgment language used by other Old Testament prophets to
describe a dramatic reordering of national prominence and authority. In
this case, the Kingdom of God is being taken away from apostate Israel and
given to people who will produce its fruit in fulfillment of Matthew 21:42-
44 - "Jesus said to them, "Have you never read in the Scriptures: "The stone
that the builders rejected has become the cornerstone; this was the Lord's
doing, and it is marvelous in our eyes'? Therefore I tell you, the kingdom of
God will be taken away from you and given to a people producing its fruits.
And the one who falls on this stone will be broken to pieces; and when it
falls on anyone, it will crush him." This is the standard understanding of
this passage by pre-twentieth century theologians.

- John Lightfoot (1602-1675) - "...the Jewish heaven shall perish, and
  the sun and moon of its glory and happiness shall be darkened –
  brought to nothing. The sun is the religion of the [Jewish] church;
  the moon is the government of the [Jewish] state; and the stars are
  the judges and doctors of both."[3]

- Thomas Scott (1832) - "The darkening of the sun and moon, the
  falling of the stars, and the shaking of the powers of the heavens,
  denote the utter extinction of the light of prosperity and privilege
  to the Jewish nation; the unhinging of their whole constitution in
  church and state; the violent subversion of the authority of their
  princes and priests; the abject miseries to which the people in
  general, especially their chief persons, would be reduced; and the
  moral or religious darkness to which they would be consigned."[4]

---

[3] John Lightfoot (1602-1675), *A Commentary on the New Testament from the Talmud and
Hebraica: Matthew-1 Corinthians* (Peabody, MA: Hendrickson Publishers, [1859 1989),
319-20
[4] Thomas Scott, *The Holy Bible Containing the Old and New Testaments, According to the
Authorized Version; with Explanatory Notes, Practical Observations, and Copious Marginal
References*, 3 vols. (New York: Collins and Hannay, 1832), 3:110

- William Dalton (1842) - "Our Savior goes on, to set forth the calamities that should befall the Jewish nation, immediately after the destruction of Jerusalem. So entire was the subversion of their ecclesiastical and civil state, that it may be metaphorically represented by the sun, moon, and stars, losing their light, and all the heavenly bodies being dissolved..."[5]

Apocalyptic Language

What we are confronted with in this section of the 'Olivet Prophesy' is apocalyptic language, and it continues in verse 30 - "Then will appear in heaven the sign of the Son of Man, and then all the tribes of the earth will mourn, and they will see the Son of Man coming on the clouds of heaven with power and great glory." At first reading, this verse seems to be describing the physical and visible return of Christ. But, notice that the 'sign of the Son of Man' is what appears, not the 'Son of Man' himself. The literal translation of this verse found in the *English Interlinear New Testament* provides a clearer understanding - "And then will appear the sign of the Son of Man [who is] in heaven and then will mourn all the tribes of the earth [γῆς-land] and they will see the Son of Man coming on the clouds of heaven with power and great glory." What Jesus is saying is that a 'sign' will be given indicating that the 'Son of Man' is in heaven. And this 'sign' will cause the tribes of the land to mourn. The 'sign' given is not in the sky [in heaven], rather the 'Son of Man' [the Messiah] has been exalted and is now in heaven. The verse ends with a line of familiar judgment language, "...they will see the Son of Man coming on the clouds of heaven with power and great glory." The verb 'will see' [ὄψονται] indicates that they will physically see and properly perceive. The Messiah [Jesus], who is in heaven, will execute judgment on apostate Israel. What is the 'sign'? It is the destruction of Jerusalem and its Temple. Christ, whom the Jewish authorities rejected, had been exalted and given power and authority to execute judgment. At Pentecost, Peter closes the first Christian sermon with this affirmation - "Let all the house of Israel therefore know for certain that God has made him both Lord [possessing all authority] and Christ [Messiah], this Jesus whom you crucified (Acts 2:36)." The destruction of Jerusalem and the Temple cultus sealed the end of the Jewish Age. Christ,

---

[5] W. Dalton, *An Explanatory and Practical Commentary on the New Testament*, 2 vols. (London: R.B. Seeley and W. Burnside, 1842), 1:118

who is the Messiah, had been enthroned in heaven and is now ruling over his Kingdom. The Messianic Age had begun in fulfillment of Daniel's prophecy -

> *"I saw in the night visions, and behold, with the clouds of heaven there came one like a son of man, and he came to the Ancient of Days and was presented before him. And to him was given dominion and glory and a kingdom, that all peoples, nations, and languages should serve him; his dominion is an everlasting dominion, which shall not pass away, and his kingdom one that shall not be destroyed (Dan.7:13,14)."*

It is important to note that the cloud motif that is frequently used in Scripture and appears here in verse 30, speaks of God's presence and is often used to indicate divine judgment. For example, Isaiah uses it in his judgment prophecy against Egypt - "...Behold, the Lord is riding on a swift cloud and comes to Egypt; and the idols of Egypt will tremble at his presence, and the heart of the Egyptians will melt within them (Isa.19:1)." Also, this is exactly what Jesus told the High Priest would happen - "But Jesus remained silent. And the high priest said to him, "I adjure you by the living God, tell us if you are the Christ, the Son of God." Jesus said to him, "You have said so. But I tell you, from now on you will see the Son of Man seated at the right hand of Power and coming on the clouds of heaven (Matt.26:63,64)."

A Season of Gospel Proclamation

This paragraph ends with the promise of a great season of gospel proclamation and ingathering - "And he will send out his angels [ἄγγελος - messengers] with a loud trumpet call [the call of the gospel], and they will gather his elect from the four winds, from one end of heaven to the other (Matt.24:31)." This same imagery is used in Isaiah 58:1, Matthew 8:10-12 and Luke 13:22-30. Adam Clarke, in his commentary on the 'Discourse' writes - "It is worth serious observation, that the Christian religion spread and prevailed mightily after this period: and nothing contributed more to the success of the Gospel than the destruction of Jerusalem happening in the very time and manner, and with the very circumstances, so particularly foretold by our Lord. It was after this period that the kingdom of Christ began, and his reign was established in almost every part of the world."[6] The church historian, Philip Schaff agrees - "Henceforth the heathen could no longer look upon Christianity as a mere sect of Judaism, but must regard and treat it as a new, peculiar religion. The destruction of Jerusalem, therefore, marks that momentous crisis at which the Christian church as a whole burst forth forever from the chrysalis of Judaism, awoke to a new sense of maturity, and in government and worship at once took its independent stand before the world...The church entered into the inheritance of Israel."[7]

A Natural Conclusion

The final paragraph of this passage forms a natural conclusion to this section of the 'Prophecy' - "From the fig tree learn its lesson: as soon as its branch becomes tender and puts out its leaves, you know that summer is near. So also, when you see all these things, you know that he is near, at the very gates. Truly, I say to you, this generation will not pass away until all these things take place. Heaven and earth will pass away, but my words will not pass away (Matt.24:32-35)." The fig tree is not a reference to the rebirth of national Israel, as some suggest; rather, it is a general reference to all the events Jesus had just described. Luke makes this clear by recording the line of text this way - "...look at the fig tree and all the trees (Lk.21:29)." Jesus is referring to a natural phenomenon, the fig tree is not a symbolic reference to Israel. The Lord's point is straightforwardly put: be alert...these events are about to unfold! In fact, Jesus says that "...this generation will not pass away until all these things take place (v.34)." These prophetic events were established by divine decree. A broadened form of the same cosmic symbolism is used in verse 35 - "Heaven and earth will pass away, but my words will not pass away." In other words, the Old Covenant world of Judaism will be destroyed, but Christ's prophetic word will not pass away!

---

[6] Adam Clarke, *Adam Clarke's Commentary on Matthew* 24:31 (1837)

[7] Philip Schaff, *History of the Christian Church: Apostolic Christianity*, vol. 1, The Great Tribulation, (Matt.24:21), sec.39 – 'Effects of the Destruction of Jerusalem on the Christian Church', par.2

CHAPTER 10

A Call to Watchfulness

U p to this point in Jesus' prophecy (vv. 1-35) we have witnessed the prediction of an unfolding season of great tribulation in Jerusalem. It is a season that would come to an end with the fall of Jerusalem and the destruction of the Temple. And Jesus said that everything he predicted would be fulfilled within the generation of his original hearers. It happened exactly as he said it would. The Temple was burned on August 10th A.D. 70 and the city was taken by the Romans on September 8th of the same year. These events came at the end of a severe siege of about three and a half years.

As horrific as the fall of Jerusalem was, the spiritual and religious reordering that is really at the heart of this national tragedy is even more profound. The Old Covenant Age had come to a close and the New Covenant Age was put in its place. Harold Fowler, in his commentary *The Gospel of Matthew*, writes - "If these cataclysmic events are correctly interpreted as applying to Israel's defeat, then it is clear that immediately after their national disaster of 70 A.D., the once-exalted, unique theocracy of Israel went into permanent eclipse as God's light-bearers before the nations. Now the Church of Christ occupies this glorious position (Phil.2:15f; John8:12; Matt.5:14f.; 1Peter2:9f.). Although Christianity would be established at a time when kingdoms, thrones and religious systems would be thoroughly shaken, it would be a Kingdom that shall never be shaken or replaced by anything better this side of glory (Dan.2:44; 7:14/ Heb.12:28). From the viewpoint of Jesus' contemporaries, the loss of Judaism's glory would be a world-shaking tragedy indeed, an eclipse. From God's point of view, however, the removal of things that can be shaken in order to establish a Kingdom that cannot be shaken is but to treat the former as obsolete. What, for Him, was already growing old was ready to vanish away even in the first century (Heb.8:13; 12:27f)."[1] The fall of Jerusalem, then, and the destruction of the Temple is to be understood as 'the great and dreadful day of the Lord' spoken of by Malachi (Mal.4:5). And, perhaps, an even more crucial understanding is that it is the ultimate visible evidence that one Age of divine history had given way to another. We have moved from the 'former days' to the 'last days'! So, the discourse gave the disciples and the first century Christians the forewarning and insight they needed in order to respond to these coming events appropriately.

Known Only to God the Father

Now, even though the events predicted would be fulfilled within the following forty years, the precise day and hour of judgment was known only to God the Father - "But concerning that day and hour no one knows, not even the angels of heaven, nor the Son, but the Father only (Matt.24:36)." This is a confirmation statement affirming the event described in verses 29&30, in which Old Testament prophetic imagery and judgment language is used indicating the presence of divine judgment. What was happening in Jerusalem was not ordinary civil and political disorder; it was God's judgment on apostate Judaism for its rejection of their Messiah. Judaism's prominence and place in the world was passing away, and it would end dramatically and decisively. This understanding is very prominent in the Apostle Paul's theology - "Yet among the mature we do impart wisdom, although it is not a wisdom of this age or of the rulers of this age, who are doomed to pass away. But we impart a secret and hidden wisdom of God, which God decreed before the ages for our glory. None of the rulers of this age understood this, for if they had, they would not have crucified the Lord of glory (1Cor.2:6-8)." Paul, like all Jews, divided history into the 'Jewish Age' and the 'Messianic Age' and he understood that the 'former Age' was passing away. And what Jesus is saying in the Discourse is that the 'days

---

[1] Harold Fowler, *The Gospel of Matthew* (Joplin, MO: College Press, 1985), 4:482.

of distress' he describes will set the stage and form the historical context for the day of judgment. This judgment would bring a decisive end to the Jewish Old Covenant Age, and only the Father knows the precise moment of that transaction. From our vantage-point, what ended in principle at Calvary was effectively and fully ended with the fall of Jerusalem and the destruction of the Temple. The sacrificial system that foreshadowed the work of Christ could no longer be practiced.

In order to illustrate and underscore the decisive and dramatic nature of the coming judgment, Jesus says that the 'days of Noah' parallel the 'coming of the Son of Man'. The normal patterns of life would continue: eating, drinking, and marriage. This was the nature of life in Noah's day until he entered the ark. The flood caught the people by surprise and "swept them all away". At this point Jesus draws a parallel - "...so will be the coming of the Son of Man. Then two men will be in the field; one will be taken and one left. Two women will be grinding at the mill; one will be taken and one left (Matt.24:37-41)." The normal patterns of life continued right up to the day Noah entered the ark and the rains came. Jesus says that the same will be true with the coming judgment event. The normal activities of life continued up to the surrounding of Jerusalem by the armies of Rome. Once Jerusalem was surrounded and the siege began there were only two categories of people; those 'taken' in judgment, and those 'left' - those spared because they had left the city.

This section of the prophecy is often misunderstood and misapplied. It is important to remember that the theme of this section is judgment: who will be judged and who will be spared. In the example of Noah's day the ones who were eating, drinking and marrying are the ones 'taken away'. The 'taken away' reference refers to judgment, not deliverance. This is exactly what happened when the 'Son of Man' came in judgment on Jerusalem. The unbelieving, those who rejected Christ, were taken away in judgment, and those who heeded the warning and left the city went on living. So this is not describing a 'secret rapture'; rather, it is a picture of the decisive and separating nature of judgment. Thomas Newton (1754) wrote - "Some shall be rescued from the destruction of Jerusalem, like Lot out of the burning of Sodom: while others, no ways perhaps different in outward circumstances, shall be left to perish in it."[2]

---

[2] Thomas Newton, *Dissertations on the Prophecies, Which Have Remarkably Been Fulfilled, and at This Time are Fulfilling in the World* (London: J.F. Dove, 1754), 379.

A Closing Admonition

The chapter ends with an admonition and a call to obedient
servanthood -

> *"Therefore, stay awake, for you do not know on what day*
> *your Lord is coming. But know this, that if the master of*
> *the house had known in what part of the night the thief*
> *was coming, he would have stayed awake and would not*
> *have let his house be broken into. Therefore you also must*
> *be ready, for the Son of Man is coming at an hour you do*
> *not expect. "Who then is the faithful and wise servant,*
> *whom his master has set over his household, to give them*
> *their food at the proper time? Blessed is that servant whom*
> *his master will find so doing when he comes. Truly, I say*
> *to you, he will set him over all his possessions. But if that*
> *wicked servant says to himself, 'My master is delayed,'*
> *and begins to beat his fellow servants and eats and drinks*
> *with drunkards, the master of that servant will come on a*
> *day when he does not expect him and at an hour he does*
> *not know and will cut him in pieces and put him with*
> *the hypocrites. In that place there will be weeping and*
> *gnashing of teeth (Matt.24:42-51)."*

The message of this closing passage can be summarized in three words –
'watchful', 'faithful' and 'wise'. Jesus instructs the disciples - specifically
Peter, James, John and Andrew (Mk.13:3) – and by extension the Apostolic
church, to stay alert to the general signs he described, and particularly the
sign of the surrounding armies, so they could escape the city (which the
Christians did). Then, there is a final admonition directed to the disciples.
They are to be 'faithful' and 'wise' servants who conscientiously carry out
their Apostolic responsibilities of nurturing and protecting those placed
under their care. If they are obedient to this call they will be entrusted
with greater responsibilities. If they misread the Lord's delayed coming
and abuse their fellow servants and live by their sinful passions they will
be severely punished (Matt.24:45-51). They would experience the same
judgment as the other inhabitants of Jerusalem.

The 'Olivet Prophecy' focuses on one of the most important events of
divine history: the destruction of Jerusalem and the Temple in 70 A.D. This

was a judgment event that fulfilled Old Testament Messianic prophecy; particularly, prophecies found in Daniel, Zechariah, Joel and Malachi. With the destruction of the Temple, the practice of the Old Testament sacrificial system was brought to an end, never to be reestablished. As 21st century Christians, we live with the expectation of Christ's second coming, an event defined by resurrection and the end of history.

CHAPTER 11

The Blessed Hope

The material presented in the 'Olivet Prophecy' is Christ's response to specific questions posed to him by his disciples. These questions are related to Jesus' statement that the Temple would be destroyed - "... Truly, I say to you, there will not be left here one stone upon another that will not be thrown down (Matt.24:2)." In other words, when would the Temple be destroyed, and what is the sign of Christ's coming in judgment and the end of the Jewish Age? Jesus restricts his comments to this inquiry alone. He does not attempt to enlarge the discussion and address questions the disciples did not ask. He makes no attempt to give any unsolicited information about the end of human history. So everything contained in the 'Olivet Prophecy' is related to the judgment event of 70 A.D, when Jerusalem and the Temple were destroyed by the Roman armies under the command of Titus. Jesus makes it plain that what was soon coming [within that generation – (v.34)] was a season of divine in-breaking, that would bring judgment on Apostate Israel for its rejection of the Messiah.

But focusing on the 70 A.D. event does not, however, suggest that there is no future coming of Christ to be anticipated and hoped for. One of the great errors of the modern church is to take positions on the extreme ends of the prophetic spectrum. Futurists tend to create speculative 'end time' scenarios based on prophecy that has already been fulfilled. Radical Preterists, on the other hand, force all 'second coming' references in the

New Testament to be related to the 70 A.D. event and conclude that there is no scriptural basis for the hope of the second coming of Christ. Both of these positions are misleading and do violence to the biblical text. The Futurists promote fiction as fact; and the radical Preterists consider fact to be fiction. Both of these extremes need to be avoided! Instead, it needs to be understood that there are prophetic statements in Scripture that find their fulfillment in 70 A.D. and others that refer to the return of Christ at the end of human history.

Prophecy and the 70 A.D. Event

For the sake of clarity, this distinction needs to be made. Perhaps, a sampling of passages that support each of these 'comings' would be helpful. The following texts are related to the 70 A.D. event:

- "When they persecute you in one town, flee to the next, for truly, I say to you, you will not have gone through all the towns of Israel before the Son of Man comes (Matt.10:23)."

- "Truly, I say to you, there are some standing here who will not taste death until they see the Son of Man coming in his kingdom (Matt.16:28)."

- "Be patient, therefore, brothers, until the coming of the Lord. See how the farmer waits for the precious fruit of the earth, being patient about it, until it receives the early and the late rains. You also, be patient. Establish your hearts, for the coming of the Lord is at hand. Do not grumble against one another, brothers, so that you may not be judged; behold, the Judge is standing at the door (Jam.5:7-9)."

- "The revelation of Jesus Christ, which God gave him to show to his servants the things that must soon take place. He made it known by sending his angel to his servant John, who bore witness to the word of God and to the testimony of Jesus Christ, even to all that he saw. Blessed is the one who reads aloud the words of this prophecy, and blessed are those who hear, and who keep what is written in it, for the time is near (Rev.1:1-3)."

What distinguishes these passages are the true time references they include. These passages carry a sense of immediacy, not imminence. The 'coming' referred to would occur soon. It should be noted that in the Revelation these time references are expressed in different ways because they are expressions of different Greek word groups. The phrase "...must soon take place" (Rev.1:1) is an expression rooted the word 'taxus' (ταχύς), meaning shortly or quickly. And the line "...for the time is near" (Rev.1:3) comes from the word group 'eggus' (ἐγγύς), translated near or at hand. In all of these verses, what is being referred to is an event that is about to take place. Soon means soon, not suddenness as some would suggest. The coming of Christ in judgment was a 'soon' certainty, not just a possibility. If the plain meanings of the words are respected and understood to be true time references, then they must refer to 70 A.D.

Prophecy and the Second Coming of Christ

But, along with these passages there is another set of 'coming' references that are not as time defined. Here are three examples:

- "whom heaven must receive until the time for restoring all the things about which God spoke by the mouth of his holy prophets long ago (Acts 3:21)."

- "so Christ, having been offered once to bear the sins of many, will appear a second time, not to deal with sin but to save [consummate his saving work] those who are eagerly waiting for him (Heb.9:28)."

- "For the grace of God has appeared, bringing salvation for all people, training us to renounce ungodliness and worldly passions, and to live self-controlled, upright, and godly lives in the present age, waiting for our blessed hope, the appearing of the glory of our great God and Savior Jesus Christ, (Titus 2:11-13)"

The coming of Christ, then, that is spoken of in the 'Olivet Prophecy' is distinguished by a definite window of time for its fulfillment. It would take place within the generation of Christ's original hearers. It is related to the 'Messianic' judgment that was soon to be executed against Jerusalem and Apostate Israel. Christ is not physically seen, but it is understood that he is present using the armies of Titus as an instrument of divine judgment (which was common to Old Testament judgment events).

However, there are other 'coming' statements in the New Testament that do not fit this profile. They speak of the future 'second coming' of Christ which has very distinct features and associations. This dramatic return of Christ at the end of human history has been affirmed and anticipated by Christians from the beginning. This hope of Christ's second coming is stated in every ecumenical Christian Creed and Confession from the second century to the present day. For example -

- (Rules of Faith, 2nd Century) - "...and his future appearing from heaven in the glory of the Father to sumup all things and to raise up anew all flesh of the whole human race...'

- (The Nicene Creed, 4th Century) - "He will come again in glory to judge the living and the dead, and his Kingdom will have no end."

- (The Apostles' Creed, 5th Century) - "...he ascended into heaven, and sitteth on the right hand of God the Father Almighty; from thence he shall come to judge the quick and the dead."

Defining Features of Christ's Second Coming

What are the defining features of Christ's second coming? At his ascension, the disciples were told that he would return physically and visibly. The announcement of the angels had to be startling and perhaps somewhat confusing - "This Jesus, who was taken up from you into heaven, will come in the same way as you saw him go into heaven (Acts 1:11)." Jesus disappeared in the 'glory cloud'; he was seen and then not seen. Was he gone forever? No. The promise was that he would return as they had seen him go...bodily and visibly. He would pass from one realm to the other through the portal of the 'glory cloud'. His return would be dramatic and it would alter the course and condition of human experience and the Cosmos forever!

Also, Christ's return is associated with resurrection, transformation [glorification], and judgment. The Apostle Paul speaks of this in 1Corinthians 15 and Philippians 3. He says that 'in fact', Christ has been raised from the dead, assuring those who are in union with him by faith that they also will experience bodily resurrection. This future resurrection and transformation of decided Christians will occur at the second coming of Christ (1Cor.15:20-23). At that moment ("in the twinkling of an eye, at the last trumpet" -1Cor.15:52) the dead in Christ will be raised and changed. The believer's body will be glorified, and it will "be like his glorious body" (Phil.3:21). Our resurrected body will be imperishable and infused with immortality (1Cor.15:53). This will be a glorious transformation! Our earthly body which is perishable [corruptible and given to decay] will be changed into a body of a different kind. It will be imperishable and incorruptable [it will not decay]. So, the body sown in death and the body raised in resurrection at Christ's second coming are related, but not the same. The one is a 'natural body' [soma psuchikon], a body suited for a natural earthly existence and powerless against decay and the forces of death. The resurrected body, on the other hand, is a 'spiritual body' [soma pneumatikon]; it's a physicality empowered by the pneuma [breath, Spirit] of God and not subject to corruptibility and death. There is an important distinction to be made here. The Greek word 'soma', translated 'body,' is not strictly a reference to our physicality; it also encompasses our psychological and emotional make-up. This radically transformed resurrected body possesses a physicality and nature that is suited for a heavenly and eternal existence. It is a body that is perfectly compliant and responsive to the presence and promptings of the Holy Spirit; a body that is free from the sinful impulses of the flesh. This being the case, the resurrected body corresponds to an environment that is free from the very presence of sin.

As human beings, then, we begin life as natural beings, thoroughly integrated and embodied souls; but we are earth-bound by nature as Adam was. However, in Christ [the 'last Adam' and the 'second man'] we will become spiritual persons dominated and enlivened by the Holy Spirit and yet, still embodied. For this reason, the Apostle Paul says, "Just as we have borne the image of the man of dust [Adam] we shall also bear the image of the man of heaven [Christ] (1Cor.15:49)" Just as we now bear in our humanity the fallen nature of Adam, in Christ we have been spiritually quickened and in resurrection we will bear the glorified humanity of Jesus (1Jn.3:2).

A third feature of Christ's future coming is that it will bring human history to a close and reveal the glory of the children of God. This was very much on the Apostle Paul's mind as he wrote to the church in Rome - "...the creation waits with eager longing for the revealing of the sons of God (Rom.8:19)." He goes on to say - "...the creation itself will be set free from its bondage to corruption and obtain the freedom of the glory of the children of God (Rom.8:21)." When Christ returns, the entire Cosmos will be liberated from its bondage to sin and death will be destroyed. At this point in divine history the end comes and the Kingdom is delivered to God the Father (1Cor.15:20-28). This is the terminal point of Christ's redemptive work. The season over which Christ now mediates and rules will reach its fullness and come to an end. Christ's redemptive work will be complete and everything, though familiar, will be utterly new.

The second coming of Christ is presented prominently in the New Testament text. It will be an event that is impossible to describe in ways that man's finite mind can fully understand. Even the human imagination cannot grasp the glory and transformational nature of the event. Nevertheless, Paul attempted to describe the event to the Corinthians and Thessalonians. He paints two very vivid word-pictures -

> *"Behold! I tell you a mystery. We shall not all sleep, but we shall all be changed, in a moment, in the twinkling of an eye, at the last trumpet. For the trumpet will sound, and the dead will be raised imperishable, and we shall be changed. For this perishable body must put on the imperishable, and this mortal body must put on immortality (1Cor.15:51-53)"..."But we do not want you to be uninformed, brothers, about those who are asleep, that you may not grieve as others do who have no hope. For since we believe that Jesus died and rose again, even so, through Jesus, God will bring with him those who have fallen asleep. For this we declare to you by a word from the Lord, that we who are alive, who are left until the coming of the Lord, will not precede those who have fallen asleep. For the Lord himself will descend from heaven with a cry of command, with the voice of an archangel, and with the sound of the trumpet of God. And the dead in Christ will rise first. Then we who are alive, who are left, will be caught up together with them in the clouds to meet the Lord in the air, and so we will always be with the Lord (1Thess.4:13-17)."*

This is glorious! This is the Christian's 'blessed hope'! Every generation of Christians, from the Apostolic period until today, has been waiting for this glorious event. Generations have come and gone, and yet we wait. Unbelievers, mockers, nay-sayers challenge our hope and we still believe. Just as the generation of Christians before the fall of Jerusalem endured the ridicule of unbelievers (2Pet.3:3,4), we are called to do the same. We are called to be faithful in this hope until the end because it is an integral part of redemption. To deny the second coming of Christ is to deny the bodily resurrection of believers. And if there is no resurrection our faith is in vain. The conviction of the Apostle Paul then is absolutely true - "If in Christ we have hope in this life only, we are of all people most to be pitied (1Cor.15:19)."

The second coming of Christ is anticipated, but the exact day of its occurrence is not known. So, we are called to be ready, to be diligent, to be faithful followers of Christ. What we do know is that Christ's return will be sudden - "...in a moment, in the twinkling of an eye,...(1Cor.15:52)." This will be the most transformative event in human history! The entire cosmos will become more glorious and our status as the children of God will take on another dimension of expression. This is when the promise of John will be fulfilled - "Beloved, we are God's children now, and what we will be has not yet appeared; but we know that when he appears we shall be like him, because we shall see him as he is (1Jn.3:2)." At Christ's return we will take on the 'image of the man of heaven (1Cor.15:49)." The temporal will give way to the eternal and the mundane will turn to glory!

And Then There's Glory

There is a very real sense in which the biblical story ends where everything begins. We are left with a promise of Christ's second coming and the resurrection of the dead in Christ and the catching away of the alive in Christ (1Thess.3:13-18). At that moment everything changes. The entire created order is 'set free from its bondage to corruption' and it enters into the 'freedom of the glory of the children of God' (Rom.8:21). The glory promised to Christian believers will then be experienced (Rom.8:18). Christ is our 'hope of glory' (Col.1:27) and it is at his second coming that this glorious hope is realized. In that event everything in the cosmos becomes more substantial; we will be overwhelmed by the weightiness of awe, and we will be reclothed in the embodiment of resurrection. Redemption will be complete and the eternal Age will begin: glorified bodies, a new heaven and a new earth, incorruptability, immortality, life everlasting!

What is so reassuring is that no believer in Christ, dead or living, will miss out on this event. The Apostle Paul assured the Thessalonians that at his coming, "the dead in Christ will rise first. Then we who are alive, who are left, will be caught up together with them in the clouds to meet the Lord in the air, and so we will always be with the Lord (1Thess.4:17)". At that moment the Apostolic promise will be fulfilled - "...those whom he predestined he also called, and those whom he called he also justified, and those whom he justified he also glorified (Rom.8:30)." The verb 'glorified' is a proleptic aorist [a prophetic past tense] indicating the certainty of the believer's glorification. Here, the future merges with the past and the present, assuring us that the decrees of God are as good as done. And what sets Christianity apart from Eastern religious thought (Hinduism and Buddhism) is that this catching away and glorification is not into disembodiment. Rather, we are "further clothed, so that what is mortal may be swallowed up by life (2Cor.5:4)". At the return of Christ the Christian believer will receive salvation in its full bodily form. And according to the Apostle Peter we can have absolute confidence in this promise because it is our "living hope"; it is our "inheritance that is imperishable, undefiled, and unfading, kept in heaven [in God's presence]" for us (1Pet.1:3,4). Our resurrection and glorious transformation is guaranteed to us because Christ has been raised from the dead!

This Christian hope is at the heart of the gospel. It is the hope of the full reversal of the futility of the Fall. At the second coming of Christ we will come full circle....back to Eden. Sin will no longer have place in the cosmic environment, death will be defeated, and Christ and life in the Spirit will reign forever and ever!

Looking Forward

The hope of the gospel looks forward as it reaches back. It is a hope grounded in real history; it appeals to the life, death, resurrection, and ascension of Christ for its sure foundation. As decided Christians our confidence in the face of death, our assurance of a more substantial life in the future is not a self-deluded dream designed to help us come to terms with our mortality. Rather, it is a sure hope embedded in the saving-sacrifice of Jesus at Calvary...a real event of history! It is a hope tied tightly to Christ's resurrection...a real event of history! It is a hope that flows from Christ's promise to return, which is as trustworthy as the life he lived!

Final Thoughts

Biblical prophecy can be confusing and difficult to understand. It has been a source of controversy and conflict in the church for centuries. Conflicting interpretations of prophecy have divided the church unnecessarily. We need to remember that the basis of our fellowship as Christians is the Lordship of Christ. We have fellowship with one another because we have surrendered to the rule of Christ, and are walking together in the light of the Gospel. We can hold differing understandings of the 'Olivet Prophecy' and still stand united!

What demonstrates authentic Christian discipleship is not our convictions regarding biblical prophecy but, rather, our love for one another. Hopefully, the thoughts presented in this book have contributed to your understanding of biblical prophecy.

To Read Further

- Adams, Jay, *The Time Is At Hand*, (Presbyterian and Reformed Publishing Co., Nutley, New Jersey, 1977)

- DeMar, Gary, *Last Days Madness*, (American Vision Inc., Atlanta, Georgia, 1997)

- Eusebius, *Ecclesiastical History*, (Baker Book House, Grand Rapids, Michigan, 1976)

- France, R.T., *Matthew, Tyndale New Testament Commentaries*, (William B. Eerdmans Publishing Company, Grand Rapids, Michigan, 1992)

- Hoekema, Anthony, *The Bible and The Future*, (William B. Eerdmans Publishing Company, Grand Rapids, Michigan, 1997)

- Josephus, Flavius, *The Complete Works of Josephus*, (Kregel Publications, Grand Rapids, Michigan, 1981)

- Kik, J. Marcellus, *An Eschatology of Victory*, (Presbyterian & Reformed Publishing Co., Phillipsburg, N. J., 1971)

- Noe, John, *Beyond the End Times*, (International Preterist Association, 1999)

- Russell, James Stuart, *The Parousia*, (Kingdom Publications, Bradford, PA., 1996)

- Thomas, Derek W. H., *Heaven on Earth*, (Christian Focus Publications, Ltd., Scotland, UK, 2018)

Printed in the United States
By Bookmasters